THE WORLD AND LANGUAGE

The Ontology for Natural Language

Alexander Mitjashin

University Press of America,® Inc.
Lanham · Boulder · New York · Toronto · Oxford

Copyright © 2006 by
University Press of America,® Inc.
4501 Forbes Boulevard
Suite 200
Lanham, Maryland 20706
UPA Acquisitions Department (301) 459-3366

PO Box 317
Oxford
OX2 9RU, UK

All rights reserved
Printed in the United States of America
British Library Cataloging in Publication Information Available

Library of Congress Control Number: 2006926147
ISBN-13: 978-0-7618-3523-3 (paperback : alk. paper)
ISBN-10: 0-7618-3523-7 (paperback : alk. paper)

∞™ The paper used in this publication meets the minimum
requirements of American National Standard for Information
Sciences—Permanence of Paper for Printed Library Materials,
ANSI Z39.48—1984

Contents

Preface	vii
Introduction	ix
The Grammar	1
The Grammar of Language and the Platonist	7
Addition	17
The Natural Numbers	21
Iterations in Formal Arithmetic	29
Numbers by Convention	33
The Continuum Hypothesis	37
The Rich Man's Argument	43
The Laws of Logic	53
Inferences	57
Summary	61

Extending Terms	63
Terms as Points	67
The Distinguishing Function	71
Other Modes of Connection	73
The Fixed Point Theorem	75
"Fixed Points" in Language	77
Wittgenstein's Language	79
"The Philosophical I"	83
The Paradox of Language	85
The Dilemma of Language	87
Another Mode of Connection	91
The Metaphysical Solution	93
The Ontological Solution	95
The External World	99
Realism Inferred	101
"Fixed Points" and Physics	103
Heraclites' Philosophy	107
The Integrated View	111
The Copenhagen Interpretation	115
Systems of Distinctions	121
Laws and Distinctions	123
Skepticism	125
Skepticism of another Form	127
Falsifiability	131

The Grammar and the Grammar	133
Entities in the Head	137
Platonism	141
Bibliography	145
Name Index	149
Subject Index	151

Preface

Being devoted to just one subject, the range of topics of this book may seem rather large. This is due to the subject itself.

It may be expressed in the following way (in the book it is presented somewhat differently). It is assumed that natural language is not linear. Linear languages are those in which an iteration of a sign is allowed. In contrast to that, in natural language, as the assumption runs, an iteration of a term must have necessarily another meaning than the initial term. The coverage of topics is due to this assumption. They are those related to non-linearity of language or its consequences.

Cogency of the notion of non-linearity is deemed to grow as its explanatory power is being revealed; though the idea of non-linearity itself does not seem to be contrary to common sense from the very beginning. Among the issues discussed, there are the following: paradoxes, the concept of number, realism (as it should be understood within the concept), falsifiability, a peculiar aspect of mind-body problem, universals and other issues.

Some of those issues may be regarded as deduced from the assumption or as being explained in its terms.

Often it happens that what is deduced has prompted what has been deduced from. As to this concept, someone could regard it as prompted by its very approach to paradoxes (logical ones, as well as semantical). I would not underestimate the import of this approach as a stimulus which could help in giving birth to the concept itself. But some might be inclined to present this approach as a certain "razor" cutting off all the concepts except for those (as, say, non-linearity itself) which are in accordance with it. Although this view might seem to be not very far from the truth, it could be recognized neither as accurate nor as very perspicacious. For, as will be seen from the text, if this work is a one-concept work, this concept is only non-linearity (or the Grammar of language).

Alexander Mitjashin
St. Petersburg , February 2006

Introduction

There are philosophers who regard language *primarily*, if not *exclusively*, as a set of propositions, or sentences, or statements. It has long since been granted that the phenomena language is to describe may be only described by sentences. Even if one does not accept without reservations the famous motto "only sentences have meaning", one, most probably, must be tacitly convinced that to explain any phenomena means to present some sentences, which are to be judged whether true or false, and to explain the world – be our explanation true or false – all we are to do and all we can do is to present some set of sentences, too.

But sentences – even propositions – are not all there is in language and is not what there is *primarily*. And if we explain the world in sentences, it does not mean that we have to do so because it is due to the world itself, i.e. that the world admits only such an explanation. That the phenomena of the world are always explained with some set of sentences cannot necessarily entail that any explanation of *language* as a phenomenon of the world should start from sentences or propositions. We can assert that the world consists of facts and those facts can be described only with sentences, but it seems we have no sufficient ground either to assert something that could be regarded as the reverse of this assertion, or to make a stronger assertion. We cannot say with certainty that facts urge natural language to be essentially sentences or that the single reason why we explain the world is our ability to utter sentences.

This book may be recommended to those who are about to object to what is said above and to those who are inclined to agree, for the author of the book, as though avoiding to raise counter-objections to receive in response some more, instead, puts forward straight away *how* language should be constructed if it is not to be done as a set of sentences. We regard language *primarily* as a set of terms.

As it seems, this attitude turns out to be fruitful enough. Having established in the first chapters the way terms of language are to be connected one to another – "grammatical connection" is one of the basic principles of the work and is laid as one of the most general notions for language, thus it is evidently more general than logical relations; we hold that a number of philosophical and logical concepts may be explained in terms of these principle notions. Language as consisting of "the distinct terms" can account for the natural numbers, logical inferences; we yield language without contradictions and without necessity of revision of the notion of truth.

The steps from language to ontology are dramatic: the concept of the realism corresponding to the concept of language is inferred through a *reductio ad absurdum*. This "realism" so inferred differs from the concepts of realism which are received in nowadays – say, from scientific realism. But as may be seen from the work, the ontology may be regarded in a certain sense opposite to the scientific picture of the world but by no means contradictory to it.

It may be regarded as opposite to the usual scientific picture of the world because of a peculiarity of the latter, which may be described as follows. To describe the world, as it must be, to obtain its true picture, we must possess the means that correspond to the world as it must be and as it is. Those means must be adequate to what there is in the world; our cognition must correspond to the content of what we learn and what we ever might learn. The world as it is to be known must constitute a certain unity; it is 'substantially unique'. It must be in a certain sense homogeneous, at least as and in so far as understandable for us. That is, traditional scientific picture presupposes (tacitly or outwardly) that our language, our mathematics, our ways to test hypotheses, our logic, is adequate to the world as it is represented in them and this world represents something that is substantially and causally whole. This picture was seriously shattered in XX-th century, especially by the explanations of the discoveries in the micro-world, but it still exist as a preconception, as something that we yet do not observe but that we must look for and rely upon, as something that still has not been replaced and whose replacement is regarded as something not so realistic.

The opposite picture that is treated in the book may be described as follows. Our language, our logic, our mathematics, provides that the world cannot be unique as a substance. Since we use our language, logic, mathematics, we can have absolutely no reason to suppose that we describe or we can ever describe a world that represents a unity, a world that can be ever reduced to the only entity in any way. We can only describe a world that contains only entities, which not only cannot be reduced to the one, but whose similarity cannot be such that one could be reduced to another or replaced by another.

The author realizes that the former preconception of the *whole* world may be deeper rooted to be rejected with the help of the concept of non-linear language, even if it is the language without contradictions, whose explanatory power may be great. This preconception disguised with metaphysical and religious beliefs had great importance for the origin and development of the Western culture. But it is not the matter of our concern. Our only subject-matter is knowledge, which is usually called *scientific,* knowledge, of which may be said that the question of its validity (falsehood or truth) may be answered by anybody, knowledge of that which can be repeated by anyone who wishes. This knowledge cannot turn out to be peculiar only to one culture or civilization; hence, we may not bother about explaining the importance or influence of this preconception.

A question that is asked very often is 'what are distinct entities?' In the case, we infer that if we recognize that our language (non-linear language) necessarily implies that the world may be only regarded as distinct entities and in no other way, then what are they ? It is hard to explain the obvious and point out everything at once. Distinct entities are just what are deduced. If we speak about ontology, we cannot explain more than ontology says. And ontology cannot give way for further explanations as it is the case with, say, physics and other sciences. Ontological entities just are not something that can be characterized further. Ontological entities must be the most general and hence, cannot be concretized. Otherwise, it would not be ontology.

The Grammar

To regard language without its division into object-language and meta-language often means to have some advantages over the regard to it within this division. It seems that the most obvious of the advantages is that in this case we are nearer to the things as they exist, for any meta-language may be derived only from language, and object-language, in the upshot, is nothing but natural language with whose help this object-language is being studied. Another advantage – for many a very dubious one – is that having natural language as object-language, it makes no sense to care about any univocality, for natural language has no univocality; that is, this is not the case that a single name is to correspond to a single entity in natural language. One-name-to-one-entity correspondence is mostly applied in constructions of different artificial languages based on natural language when one wishes to obtain an exact language.

Unlike some (hypothetical) artificial language, natural language itself is constructed in such a way that it need not have a single name (word or expression) for a single entity (object or concept). And this is not difficult to verify. Any natural language is full of words sounding similar which have different meanings and words which sound differently having the same meaning. Despite the fact that some natural languages are merely overcrowded by words of this or the other kind, no serious misunderstanding or difficulties of expression ever arise.

Thus if we confront a word which can have another meaning, we ask our interlocutor which of the meanings he means or try to find out which of the meanings suits the context. If we hear about a "game", we usually have no problems to learn whether this concerns gambling, a contest or a hunted animal; if we are informed about somebody who is a bachelor, we can guess from the circumstances whether it is meant that he is a single man or that he is scholared;

we always know when "jungle" is a forest and when it is a struggle for survival. Hardly anyone who masters a language finds it cumbersome or superfluous to have at his disposal synonyms designating a single entity, applying different synonyms in different circumstances or contexts "commence", though, it stands for the same as "begin", traditionally is able to stress the solemnity of a case; choosing between "shuffle" or "reorganization" may depend on the position it brings you.

We are entitled to say that if a word may have different meanings, i.e. if a word designates not one but different entities, we are able to determine which entity is meant with the help of the context the word is in. And we may also say that if there are several words to designate a single entity, different words designating this single entity may be used in different contexts. Note that unlike the former, the latter is not necessary. To determine what entity is meant we have to have the corresponding context, but in general we may choose any synonym.

Is there any principle or rule, existing on the objective level that allows us to understand why natural language need not have a necessary correspondence of a single entity with a single word? ("On the objective level" means that it must be inherent to language, constitutive to it, a principle that language has in its construction, without which language would not be language.)

We argue that such principle exists. And since we also argue that this principle is the crucial for language, we could try to show that it can be presented actually in any terms. We could, for instance, explain it in terms of the notion of *definition*.

Thus, we argue that a sign in a natural language has meaning when it is followed (or may be followed) by other signs necessarily different from it; and in case any meaning is to be contributed at all, other *different* signs are to be added. Thus adding to a sign a sign different to it, we alter its meaning if it has any.

It may be said that a sign that cannot be followed by a sign different from the former is no sign of a language, for it has no definition (no meaning) in the language. (Of course, this is no extensional statement). If a definition is circular, i.e. if what is defined appears in the definition, the definition must be considered failed, and what is to be defined has no meaning in language. If we call it "nonsensical", this means that we ascribe it a meaning, for in this case "nonsensical" is different from the word which is thus defined. We can also say that changes in some meaning can be done through adding to the meaning some signs which are different both from the sign whose meaning we are trying to correct (or enlarge) and from the signs of which consists the meaning in question.

We are stating that signs of natural language (words, expressions or terms – anything to which a meaning may be ascribed, or may be intended to be ascribed) are meaningful (in the broad sense of the word, in the sense which has been just meant) only if they are (or may be) followed (or are somehow connected to) by different signs (signs, distinct from the former). Only adding different signs do we make other meanings.

Can we now generalize this statement? Can we make this statement looser and say that it is the characteristic property of natural language? Can we say that terms of language are distinct, i.e. one can be distinguished this or that way from another? In general all terms of language must look like this:

A B C D E F G....

If the signs of natural language happen to look as the following:

A B C D A F G....

.... ,

then they can be presented this way:

A B C D A^d F G....

....

....

or this way:

A B C D A^f F G....

or any other way provided that A at the beginning of the series must be (or may be) distinguished from A inside the series. Thus if the signs have no order, and if some signs seem the same, they nevertheless must be distinguished in language (simply because they are signs of language):

    D   C   A
    B A   GF

may be turned into, say:

    D C
    B   G F
      AA*

No matter how many same signs there are, language is constructed in such a way that it contains no fewer means to distinguish them (in the above example those "means" have provided us with the signs *, d, f).

According to this view, language is not simply something like a set of signs intended for communication, but it is something like a mechanism or an algorithm (in a very general sense) which turns each of its sign (of finite number) into something different from another. How can it be realized in natural (finite) language that its signs are distinct from each other? Terms of language may be invented, new words may be introduced; and new terms may be composed through the grammatical connections of old terms one to another. Thus our series, which now looks like this:

A B C D E F G * d f,

may be enlarged:

A, B, AB, C, D, E, DEA, F, BF, G,*, AD*F, d, f, Adf*, *DAGf ....etc.

All the above terms, both initial, i.e. consisting of a single sign, and composed of those single signs are allowable in language, for they are distinct as terms: A is distinct from AB, and AB is distinct from B, etc.

If natural language is such that terms must be distinct, should it mean that grammatical connecting of the same signs is not allowed?

Given the terms A, B, C, ... we can compose the terms ABC, AC, AB, BC, .., but can we also compose the terms AA, BB, CC, ...? Evidently language can contain no prohibitions for an iteration of a term, and, generally speaking, terms consisting of the same, identical terms are not considered nonsensical or meaningless. But it does not contradict the assumption that terms of natural language must be distinct. For one and the same term may be iterated, i.e. grammatically connected to itself, but it does not mean that it will have the same meaning that the single term (i.e. the term initial to the term consisting of iterated terms) has. Thus the term AA has another meaning than the term A; in other words, it can designate anything but what the term A can designate. Terms of language, such as

A B C D E F * e f AC A D CDFE A*C Ae .... etc.

are distinct from each other and terms like AA BB CC.... occurring among them are as different from A B C (correspondingly) as they are different from AB BC AC.... or any other.

As our assumption on the distinct terms runs, the real grammar of language requires that terms must be different independently of whether they "literally" are so or not. In language once something is grammatically connected to something, this must be considered different from the other. The grammatical connection is making anything different from what it is connected to, no matter how it is designated or what it is denoting. The grammatical connection in the broad sense is nothing but indicating the difference of the connected. This may seem not worthy of attention or trivial when connected terms are evidently distinctive of each other, but one might object to this when terms to be connected are the same – this might look as the refutation of the thesis. Meanwhile we would rather call "synonyms" AA and AC (or, for example, A and B), but we could never make synonyms of AA and A.

And this is actually so. Let us equate the term A with "table", and for the term B with "two". Then given the order of the terms to be arbitrary, we infer that "table and table" (AA) are "two tables" (AB), on the other hand, we shall never call "table and table" (AA) a "table" (A). We never say that AA is A except for elliptical cases; that is, we never mean that AA is A. If you talk about the boss of your boss, you do not mean that this is just your boss; what you really mean – even if you just call him "boss" – is that the boss of your boss is the boss of your boss, and your boss is nothing but your boss. And if one owns up that all his income consists of the interest rate of his savings, he does not mean that this is the income of the interest rate of the interest rate (at least he should not).

Explaining our assumption, we have said that a term has a meaning if it is grammatically connected to other terms, the ones which are different from that term. This assertion must not be taken for the one to have some meaning-theoretical content.

To say that a sign is to be followed by signs which are different from the sign is not to determine what *is* meaning. This means only to point out what we are doing when we ascribe a meaning to a sign whatever we understand as "meaning". Taking any theory – meaning may be understood as sense and reference, or use, or we may support that meaning is what a sentence has according to the truth-conditions of its constituents, or that meaning is developing along with our knowledge of whose the meaning is, i.e. "natural kinds", or we may insist that meaning is in the head, as it is the case in philosophy of mind – we could not avoid assigning signs different to the sign whose meaning is to be determined.

The Grammar of Language and the Platonists

The thought that (generally speaking) if we make up a term doubling a single term through a grammatical connection, we cannot treat the former and the latter as equal is convincingly illustrated in logical paradoxes.

Logical paradoxes were discovered in Cantor's set theory. Cantor developed a theory where some abstract mathematical problems were treated, such as the problem of infinity, and the base of the theory was the notion of a set. A set is simply any unification of definite and quite distinguishable objects in our perception or thought. Even this clear and evident definition was unrecoverably undermined by Russell. He discovered a contradiction in this simple notion, which had serious consequences - the immediate one was that Frege decided that his construction of arithmetic based on set theory was a failure.

According to Cantor's definition, a set is determined by its members, i.e. by the elements of the set. For instance, a set is the set of even numbers, the set of mammals or any other collection of objects. Sets may be themselves elements of sets, thus the set of integers has sets as its elements. The major part of sets are not their own elements; thus, the set of cats is not its own element, for the set itself is by no means a cat. But sets belonging to themselves are possible - for instance the set of all sets.

Let us regard the set of all sets which are not members of themselves. Is it a member of itself? It is a member of itself since it consists of sets - being a set it consists of sets. But if so, it is not a member of itself, for it is the set of all sets which are not members of themselves. In any case it is a member of itself and it is not a member of itself. (Russell's paradox).

Grammatically connected terms alter their initial meaning. In particular, a term grammatically connected to a similar term does not mean what the initial (the single) term does: AA can never be A. In particular, a set of sets can never be a set. AA may be anything but A; AA is only AA (or signs that we can choose to stand for AA), and A is only A. So a set of sets is a set of sets, and a set is a set; but a set of sets is not a set. Thus we conclude that though the set of all sets which are not members of themselves has sets (sets which are not members of themselves) as its members, it cannot be a member of itself since it is not a set (it is the set of all such sets). On the other hand, members of members are no members – only members of members are members of members and members are members. Sets which are not members of themselves consist of (have as members) objects which cannot be sets. Those objects can be nothing but members of members as regards the set of all sets which are not members of themselves. So the set of all sets which are not members of themselves cannot be a member of itself by the reason that, firstly, it has sets (viz. sets which are not members of themselves) as members, but it is no set; and, secondly, objects which are members of all sets which are not members of themselves are members of its members, which makes impossible for the set of all such sets to be referred to as simply "member of itself".

So it seems clear that, had it been realized that there were a sharp distinction between the set of all sets and sets proper, between members of members and members proper, that to confuse the two notions must not be allowable, the contradiction could not be formed.

Naturally, someone who knows that two of the same grammatically connected terms must be distinguished from the single term is to expect from a theorist who encounters in his theory the term "the set of such and such sets" that he introduces a new definition for the term "a set of sets", a definition that differs from the definition of "a set".

Another set-theoretical paradox concerns the notion of cardinal numbers. A cardinal is an abstraction from the nature of members of a set and from their order. A cardinal is the set of all sets whose members may be set into one-to-one correspondence. For instance, if we correlate the set of three cats, three mammals and three natural numbers in the fashion one element to one element of each set, then we yield the cardinal number 3.

A cardinal is less than another if and only if all its elements can be one-to-one-correlated to a subset of another cardinal, but this latter cardinal cannot be one-to-one correlated with any subset of the former.

The set of subsets of a set is the set which can be formed from the set. That is, the set (1, 2, 3) can form the sets (1), (2), (3), (1, 2), (1, 3), (2, 3) – the proper set (1, 2, 3) can be included as its own subset. Cantor's theorem says that the cardinal of a set is always less than the cardinal of its subsets, e.g. the one-to-one correlation of 1, 2, 3 and (1), (2), (3), (1, 2), (1, 3), (2, 3), (1, 2, 3) cannot be realized. And the paradox runs:

Let there be the set of all sets. As such, it must contain the set of its subsets – hence the cardinal of the set of its subsets must not be greater than its own cardinal. But according to Cantor's theorem, the cardinal of the set of subsets of any set must be greater than the cardinal of the set.
Thus, the contradiction.

It really makes sense to say that unlike in the case of a set, the set of all sets must include the set of its subsets, therefore concluding that the cardinal of the set of all sets is the biggest. The set of all sets, as a set of sets, must have another definition than the set, and hence other characteristics and properties. Regarding this, it is not correct that the cardinal of the set of all sets must be necessarily less than the cardinal of the set of all the subsets of the set of all sets, for Cantor's theorem has been proved for the set, but it has never been proved for the set of all sets. It was proved that a set should have a lesser cardinal than the set of its subsets, then an entity was encountered whose characteristic – the characteristic which might pass for the definition – was that its cardinal is bigger than the one of all its subsets, viz. all the sets, since this is the set of all sets. This is evident from the very formulation of the paradox. Nevertheless the notion of the set and the notion of the set of all sets are preferred to be deemed equal and Cantor's theorem to be applicable to the latter notion, too.

To be convinced that Cantor's theorem was proved just for the set, we should refer to the extract where Quine exposes one of the easiest versions of the proof. Calling sets "classes" and elements "cows" Quine is showing that no correlation of cow classes to cows accommodates all the cow classes in the following way (1976 p.14):

> Suppose a correlation of cow classes to cows. It can be any arbitrary correlation; a cow may or may not belong to the classes correlated with her. Now consider the cows, if any, that do not belong to the classes correlated with them. These cows themselves form a cow class empty or not. And it is a cow class that is not correlated with any cow. If the class were so correlated, that cow would have to belong to the class if and only if she did not.

It is immediately seen that the proof is provided for a set, but not for "the set of all sets" that should include whatever appears, e.g. the set of objects correlated to sets, the members of the set do not belong to. It seems obvious that to state the same of the set of all sets requires a special proof. It would be interesting to notice Quine's remark that the proof is suffused "with distinct air of a paradox" (1976). Within the line of our assertion that logical paradoxes arise as a result of mistaking of an iterated term for a non-iterated term – which must be different in the language of the distinct terms, we shall try to reveal where this air could come from. Let us call cows which do not belong to the classes they are correlated with "vacantly correlated". If that class is correlated with any cow, the cow must be vacantly correlated to the vacantly correlated cows. But we do not know what is to be vacantly correlated to something vacantly correlated; we do not know at all what "a correlation for correlation" is. The only definition at our disposal is the definition of one-to-one correlation, and this is a different notion than a correlation for correlation. Thus, within the given definition we cannot state the existence of such a cow.

Suppose a relation R, such as for any two elements a and b, whether aRb or bRa or a=b; for two elements a and b there is only one of the relations aRb, bRa, a=b; from aRb and aRc follows aRc. Any subset of the set within the relation has a "first" element, e.g. such is the element 1 in the set of natural numbers, and it is the predecessor of all the others. This relation is called well-ordering, and the set with this relation is a well-ordered set. According to Cantor's concept, ordinals are equivalence classes (sets with the relations between one another as the relation of equality: a=a; if a=b, then b=a; if a=b and b=c, then a=c) of well-ordered sets in accord to the existence of one-to-one correlation preserving the ordering.

The notion of ordinals generated the paradox (Burali-Forti):

If we order according to magnitude all the ordinal numbers which are smaller than a given ordinal number a, then the ordinal number of the resulting well-ordered set is a. Consider now the well-ordered set S of all the ordinal numbers arranged by magnitude. If its ordinal number is W, then every ordinal number in the given set is smaller than (and therefore different from) W, which contradicts the hypothesis that S contains all the ordinals.

But obviously, W is not constructed as an ordinal (or as all ordinals are done). W is distinctly constructed as the ordinal of the well-ordered set of all ordinals. All the ordinals are smaller than W, i.e. all the ordinals are smaller than the ordinal of all ordinals. There is no ground to state that W is on some magnitude rank among the ordinals of S, as there is no ground to say that W is just an ordinal. The formulation of the paradox implies that the mode ordinals are given – the ordinal number *a* is the one of the well-ordered set of ordinals smaller than *a* – can be adopted by the construction of the ordinal of well-ordered set of all ordinals. The single reason to place W among the ordinals of S would be the term "ordinal" in its name, viz. "the ordinal of the well-ordered set S of all ordinals". But in accordance with our assumption that the Grammar of language implies connection of the distinct terms, repeating of a term is making another term, e.g. "the ordinal of such-and-such ordinals" is no ordinal.

The thought that the set of all the sets which do not belong to themselves is no set or the set of all the sets is no set, or the ordinal of the set S of ordinals is no ordinal, is not a novelty. Rather this was the first that occurred to the theorists in their attempts to avoid contradictions.

The last paradox that was exposed here, Burali-Forti's, historically was the first that was discovered in the general set theory. On its appearance it encounters Cantor's reaction. Cantor pointed out the necessity to separate notions of sets and notions of "too big sets"; that is, manifolds which are at the same time "unities" and others that cannot consistently be thought as "unities", the "inconsistent manifolds". But a mere assertion that these should be rejected is not acceptable. Some definite procedure is needed for distinguishing sets from these "inconsistent manifolds". Consequently what is needed is to write down explicitly all the principles according to which sets are to be constructed, then, of course, we would possess a definite method of distinguishing sets from the "inconsistent manifolds". These principles appeared as axioms in Zermello set theory. And the construction of sets supported by the axioms was close to the construction of sets in Cantor's theory. The sets existing in the axiomatic set theory are determined by their elements; they are equal only if their elements are equal. If some elements of a set possess some property, there exists a set possessing this property – a subset of the set. If there is one or two given objects, there is a set whose members (elements) are exactly these objects. For any set there is a set consisting of all members of members of the given set. There is at least one infinite set, viz. the natural numbers. For any set there is a set of all its subsets. For all disjoint sets there is a set which has as its members, just a single member from each set (this statement has other versions, one of them is that any set may be well-ordered). All members of a set may be altered in a unique way, if possible, which forms another set, replacing the given.

In such a system a set may be formed in the mode given in axioms and in no other mode (the axioms in our exposition are much nearer to common sense than to rigor). And this provides absence of contradictions. There are no paradoxes because there are no permissions for the existence of what makes them arise, i.e. "huge manifolds". In this formal system there can be found formulas denoting, for instance, the property of not belonging to itself, but as it is evident from the axioms, a formula denoting this property could not be applied to form a set; as well, no axiom could be regarded as allowing the application of all the sets to form a set, i.e. the set of all sets. Limiting the formation of sets by the axioms which exclude "sets" leading to contradictions is the way for this theory to be consistent.

Looking at the axioms we notice that there can be a great number of properties (predicates) which allows forming subsets in sets, e.g. having the set of natural numbers we can focus on evens or primes, etc.... There can be many ways (functions) to choose a single element from each given set to form another set; for instance, the element may be the least element in terms of relations within each of the given sets. Also there are many ways to alter elements of a set to form another set (infinitely many functions whose arguments are the elements of the given set and values are the elements of the set to be formed). These are axiom schemata. This gives us the possibility to introduce other sorts of variables ranging over predicates in these axiom schemata, as well as we have variables over members of sets in the axioms of this formal system. It is done this way in another theory of sets, that of Neumann-Bernays-Goedel. This theory is regarded as extension of Zermello's theory. Two sorts of variables form sets and, on the other hand, classes. Sets are elements and classes are non-elements – a class cannot be an element of something. Hence the way to avoid paradoxes: entities occurred in paradoxes are not sets, but classes.

Russell in his theory of types adheres to the line of solving the problem of contradictions which does not look akin to the one limiting the extension of the notion "set" or distinguishing notions "set" and "class". Russell's world is objects, relations and attributes. Objects are formally represented as arguments and attributes or relations are represented as "propositional functions". Arguments occurring in propositional functions form sentences. Then the totality of all the sentences is settled in such an order that the denial of an argument comes after the argument, the conjunction of two arguments comes after these arguments, the generalization of an argument comes after the argument etc.... This hierarchy is called "types". Russell requires that the type of a propositional function must exceed the type of the argument. Thus if we formally represent the predicate "belonging to itself" (or "not belonging to itself") talking about some entity, we break the order of consecutively ascending types, for we have to put the entity "itself" into the propositional function of higher order. In the theory of types such formulas are rejected as meaningless.

In Russell's world besides objects, attributes, relations, there are also attributes of attributes, relations of relations, relations of those relations of relations etc.... An edifice was constructed which was then amended, being simplified. Actually this world is many worlds – each for some types. Thus, to form a set one should draw a member only from one type. This way unique entities are to be multiplied: there are to be some empty sets, some replicas of each number (if not infinitely many of those entities), identity function is not unique, identical to itself, identity function, but there are arbitrarily many such; infinitely many instances of the formulas of the law of non-contradiction in the absence of contradictions.

We regard the Grammar of language as the connection of its terms, the result of which is the difference of each of the terms to each other. One of the basic ideas of the theory of types is that the type of attributes or relations must exceed the type of arguments. Thus, for given arguments, if we introduce some characteristics, attributes of those arguments, or some relations – some mode of connection between them, i.e. a certain grammar; then thereby we provide the hierarchy, a mode of sharp difference between parts of the sentences which have been so yielded (or between terms, or sorts of terms). The world is cleft into different worlds since arguments are connected within such-and-such relations or such-and-such relations of relations, then within other attributes or relations, relations of relations etc.... Connections are not to be realised in the mode of each to each, uniquely. Nevertheless contradictions are avoided. As to the Grammar of language, if something is connected, it is distinct; as to the idea of the theory of types, if something is not "distinct", it must not be connected (thus, in this formal theory, to put it roughly, such expressions as "ââ" and "not ââ" – they can constitute a paradox – are devoid of sense). What in the Grammar is of another meaning, in the theory of types is meaningless.

Quine's New Foundations is conceived as a combination of assets of Zermello's system and Russell's theory of types. Quine's system has a universal class, as in the theory of types; it has also a complement, unlike in Zermello's system, where those notions are not provided by the axioms; and unlike in Russell's system formulas may be formed without fear to render them meaningless. This is achieved by stratification, i.e. a technical device that makes variables of a formula be put with numerals in some systematic way. The device resembles Russell's theory, but it provides no types with such weaknesses as notions' reduplications. Formal analogue of the predicate "the set of all entities such that" is construed as effective only when it is applied to a stratified formula. But unstratified formulas still remain meaningful. Thus the expression standing for "not belonging to itself" can be constructed in the system and belongs to its formulas, but it is not applicable to form a set in the system.

We say that an iteration of a term is not that term. In particular, "set of sets" is not a set. Formal set theories say that such entities as "set of sets" cannot be formed as sets in the theories where sets are to be formed – in the theories where such entities are formed at all, they are not formed as sets, they are formed as other entities (viz. "classes" which must not be elements, unlike "set"). We say that the Grammar – connection of the terms of language – is what makes the connected terms distinct (a set of sets is not a set). Formal theories, to put it roughly, say that the mode of connection is such that symbols which are connected must be differently ranked in the connection, or their connection must be followed by marks or numerals to differentiate the same symbols taking different places in the connection.

Thus we should be in the right if we infer that, in order to construct a formal theory without contradictions, the theorists state, on the extensional level, that the set of such-and-such sets is not a set (or the ordinal constructed for all the ordinals is no ordinal); and, on the intensional level, they implies that the question of contradictions is the question of the grammatical connections of the symbols.

Taking into consideration that we have assumed the grammatical connection to be differentiation of the terms, we should be in the right to infer that in such extensions of natural language as the formal theories, the theorists have to state that the set of sets is not a set; and they have to imply that the question of contradictions lies in certain grammatical connections. In our view such conclusions made by the theorists are inevitable. If a theorist encounters expressions with iterated notions and which contain contradictions, it would be natural to expect that he eventually comes to the conclusion that whether the iterated notion is not the same as that notion (or if you iterate the notion, it is not the same as the initial one), or the iteration itself (more generally, connection of one to another) must be provided with an order or rules of correct applications – what we are saying is that connection is altering, i.e., in a sense, cancelling iterations.

All these conclusions in question concern formal theories. It is asserted that a formal theory must be constructed in such-and-such way, so that certain notions – namely those denoted by expressions in natural language where a notion occurs twice – must not belong to the expressions of the theory, or have any meaning or have any mode to be formed in the theory. Set theorists always tacitly imply or explicitly assert that ambiguity, impreciseness and contradictions are inherent to natural language; and for this very reason their task should be to oust contradictions out of formal theories leaving natural language intact. This approach is reassured by the existence of semantical paradoxes (Ramsey F.P. (1926) divides paradoxes into two groups: logical (i.e. set-theoretical) and semantical (others)). This seems a plausible reason why we see no endeavour to assert outright that an expression containing an iterated notion should be of another definition than this notion be single; though, as we saw, this was actually done; that is, the definitions were introduced, e.g. that of "class".

But despite what was said above, we suppose there is another, more serious motive to regard mistakenly a term and the term iterated in some grammatical connection as a single one, ascribing to the term and the iterated term one and the same meaning. This reason is a certain subliminal (but it is not excluded that it is sometimes quite conscious) Platonism.

What we call "Platonism" is the view that words of language, or notions, strictly stand for entities. This is a deeply inveterate opinion that words are something like "universals" which designate the very things, properties, relations and ideas; the latter are entities or unities of the world, its composed parts. This view cannot imply that a grammatical connection could destroy (change) the meaning of a word, for this is not the way of entities of the world to be so destroyed. "Universals" cannot be changed by mere connection, for the composite world would remain intact after this kind of connection had been done. Thus, "universals" in their integrity are what the world is, and the concept of set was supposed to be one of the key parts of this picture.

A philosopher of ancient times who criticized the concept of platonic universals, said: "What I see is no horseness, this is a horse" – for a Platonist a horse is firstly horseness, i.e. horseness is prior to a horse. In the same sense the theorists regard a set as "setness" rather than a set. The way a Platonist's speculations seem to run is the following. Let us define the concept of "a set". This allows constructing of various sets. For instance, the set of integers (a set was defined, and the set of integers is no doubtly a set), the set of evens (the set of evens is a set), the empty set (the empty set is a set), the set of all cats (the set of all cats is a set), the set of all sets (the set of all sets is a set) – "the set of sets" is to be "a set" for the same reason as "the set of cats" is. It seems that for a Platonist a set is "setness" because "set" *in general* contains all its possible characteristics, as well as "horse" *in general* does. "Of all sets" is supposed to be a characteristic of a set – a kind of its members, for a set is characterized by its members; that is why it is a set – as any other characteristic, e.g. as "cats". "Setness" would not be broken even if the members, so to say, of the "set" of "setness" were "sets" themselves, as it seems.

The consequences of this Platonism – the consequences of the view, that as a "universal", "set" must be equal to itself within any expression, beside any predicate (a universal must not undergo any altering in its meaning) – were removed from formal theories. "Huge manifolds" or incorrect constructions are not permitted in them or are meaningless – but, as it seems, this does not concern natural language, earlier reputed as ambiguous and contradictory.

Thus an implicit recognition of Platonism is held, even at the price of allowing contradictions in natural language.

It is clear that actually "the empty set", "the set of integers", "the set of all cats" etc. cannot be replaced by "set" in any predicate without the risk of making it erroneous. Their relations are those of genus and species. As for the notion "the set of all sets", it seems that even a strong belief of platonic character that this notion could be replaced by "a set" for the reason that both notions represented the same entity should be rejected as false or doubtful. For there can hardly be found an example concerning real life, not abstract constructions, where an expression with an iterated notion designates the same as this notion does. Thus, a rich man whose accrual of richness is measured not only with an interest rate but also with an interest rate of the interest rate will never identify his interest and his interest upon interest. Unlike the Platonists caught in abstract speculations, he knows very well and physically senses that all the interests on his assets are one thing – say, investments – and (average) interest on all the interests is another thing – say, expenses for his blessed living. In contrast to the case of "the set of all sets" there won't possibly be any glimpse of the idea that interest on all interests may be treated in some sense or other as interest (implicitly for the reason that this is also some "interest") – this is absolutely excluded. The rich man need not be prompted to search for another definition for the notion "interest on interest" – as is done with a theory being constructed, where some new notion arises by way of applying twice a notion already defined. For both he and his banker operate with the interest in the way it is to be treated, and operate with the interest on interest accordingly in the other way. It does not matter which operations they consider as concerning interest on interest (what exactly they mean by the interest on interest). But if any operations concern interest on interest, they must be just different from those concerning "interest" proper (e.g. if he invests the interest he gets a special rate, different from that of the interest proper, thereby the rate may be calculated as of the sum of the interest invested and the capital or separately, or whatever). Other approaches would lead to failure, which, in a sense, is tantamount to the arising of contradictions in a theory.

In real life if we repeat something, we never come to mean the same as that which has been repeated meant (for we *have* already *repeated* it).

Addition

We started our speculations by asking why language is not univocal — words and things are not in one-to-one correspondence, one and the same word does not necessarily designate one and the same thing and a thing does not necessarily have one name. Univocality is one of the "doors" to open to take on the subject we are treating, we have chosen it haphazardly.

Now it is clear that language need not be univocal. For to alter while connect means, in particular, to correct. If grammatical connecting is necessarily altering, there is the possibility to make what is fuzzy, erroneous or ambiguous less fuzzy, correct, straight or more or less clear. In reverse, there is nothing absolutely clear. Consequent altering may possibly make fuzzy or doubtful what has been clear. It does not literally mean that natural language is principally vague, as some philosophers say. Rather altering by the grammatical connection equally provides assertions on its vagueness or clarity.

The definiendum should not be smuggled into definiens, but the Grammar - the thesis that terms of language are distinct; if they appear to be the same, they must have different meaning - is by no means a simple generalization of it. Rather this is the other way round. From the assumption that terms are distinct, follows that the term to be defined must not be contained among the ones connected to the term as those to define it. For - this follows from the assumption - the iterated term means anything but what the defined (single) term should mean. The definition fails because of the iteration. What is to be defined fails to be done, for its iteration requires another definition, the one different from that of the single term.

Thus, the rule that the definiendum must not be in definiens is not a self-justified product of common sense. This is a derivation from the Grammar of language, from the thesis that to be grammatically connected means to be distinct. If the definiens is AB, the definiendum must not be A; for the expression AAB, according to the Grammar, cannot be the expression of the definition (the definiendum together with the definiens) of A, it can be anything but A.

Consequences may be not convincing, for they may be considered as particular cases or occasional phenomena. Thus, some may regard the "similarity" of the idea of the distinct terms and the solutions which could be given for the paradoxes arisen in formal theories as coincidence. Some may cast doubt on regarding the prohibition of smuggling the definiendum into definiens as derived from the idea of the Grammar. It may happen also that someone finds unimportant or not deserving attention that a derivative of derivative can *never* be deemed as just a derivative – though when the derivative of a variable is meant, this view leads to the explicit result $0=1$.

It seems that if there is a need for something decisive, something which is able to convince in indisputability of the fact that an iterated notion cannot mean what the notion does, then, the best that can be done is to indicate the natural numbers or counting.

Let us take, for simplicity, objects which are similar to the terms of language, i.e. finite and definite, those which may be simply counted – like trees and bees, not like ratios of circles and diameters or elementary particles, avoiding more complex calculi than the God-given natural numbers give. If we do distinguish one object from another, we mark their characteristics or properties, e.g. we may mark trees by form of their leaves. If we do not distinguish objects by their characteristics, nor are we able to give them any special marks, we may count them, i.e. we may give them marks which can be applied to distinguish any objects of the world regardless of any characteristics – thus, if we have in the lump oaks and maples and we should distinguish one oak from another or one maple from another, we need not firstly distinguish oaks and maples and then distinguish (by other characteristics than leaves) oaks one from another and maples one from another; we may distinguish one oak from another or one maple from another by counting (assigning numerals) oaks and maples in the lump. The nature of the natural numbers is such that once an object is identified as such, simply as an object, it can be counted (marked by a natural number "one", "two"..), even if we cannot tell of it anything but that it is an object; that is, if we cannot tell the way it differs from other objects. In reverse, objects by their very nature are those which are amenable to counting – we always can say whether there is one, two or any number of objects (if something is not countable, we refer to it in singular, as one entity, one object). This is usually supposed to be incontestable. It cannot occur to anybody to call two objects "one" in the same sense.

If we have no idea (or have no wish to have any idea) what a sign means, we are treating it as an object. But generally we distinguish signs (words, terms) one from another by their meanings. Even if signs look similar they must be considered different if they have different meanings. If the meaning is the same, two (or more) signs must be considered to be the same, even if they look similar. It may be said that, in general, signs are the same if and only if they mean the same. (We determine "sign" this way because we wish to stress the mode signs differ from other entities or objects – they must have meaning. Commonly we say "this is another word (sign) for the same" or "this may signify another thing", but in this case we actually imply that signs (i.e. what has meanings) may have various (or identical) appearances).

It is clear that the assertion that the meaning of a term which is iterated in some grammatical connection is equivalent to the term proper (not iterated) is another way of saying that the law of addition (or natural numbers) is not applicable to signs. The one who says that an iterated sign (a sign composed of two same signs) may mean the same as the sign to which the same sign has been grammatically connected actually says that the laws of arithmetic are not applicable to semantics.

So it seems, a person who denies that an iterated notion is not the initial one must go so far in justification of his view as to construct a semantics which is not subjected to the laws of arithmetic, a semantics which states that a word that defines something cannot be identified once duplicated, a semantics which treats that, unlike objects, no repeating of a word makes it be two – it always would mean the same. This might be regarded as the consequences of the view which we have called Platonism. This view might imply that objects can be counted, but "objects" never can – this might seem natural for such a Platonist. For him a derivative and a derivative, or a derivative of a derivative may be different from a derivative only by the reason that they are objects, but he could refuse to multiply the notion of "derivative".

The concept of the Grammar consists in rejecting this kind of differentiation between words and objects. It sees no reason or need to place such a restriction on the range of application of arithmetic. An object and (or) another object are not that object (they are two objects or the second object) and a term and a term are not that term, for terms are nothing but what designates objects (or entities).

It is hardly possible to conceive semantics which generally admits meanings of terms to remain the same after the terms have been multiplied, for entities meant by the terms are never the same (never remain the only ones) when multiplied.

The Natural Numbers

We have said that whatever a meaning-theoretical attitude might be, we are to connect only distinct signs (whether they look the same or not) to the sign whose meaning it is. Connecting alters the meaning; further distinct signs give another sense. But what can be said about reference?

We have asserted that grammatically connected terms must be distinct, but terms and their referents differ too. A sign differs from the sign it is connected to and differs from the object it designates. In a sense to mean is the same as to construct expression or statement, i.e. to assign something different.

A word is different from its definition just as the definiendum from definiens. And a word is different from the object it designates just as it is, as not the object. If a sign were not different from what it designates, it would not make sense to designate that. For symbols are more suitable to deal with than objects themselves. Thus, to say "horse" is for the most part more convenient than to show a horse – which is the so called ostensive definition, i.e. simply pointing out the object – or to use the notion of "emotional breakdown" is better than to make someone experience it.

All the Grammar of language implies is that expressions and sentences may be substituted only for terms which are not contained in those sentences and expressions. AB may be substituted for C. AA may be substituted for D. But AB can be substituted neither for A nor for B (it can be done, though, elliptically, as the subject's wish, not in the way language is constructed; e.g. as one may call a female fox simply "fox" or "female" in some circumstances or context). And AA can never be substituted for A without a risk of lapsing into making a mistake. Designation is of the same nature as the Grammar of language. Signs are what replace objects and they are necessarily different from objects. Thus, in language, terms differ from what they designate and terms differ one from another. This way the thesis of the Grammar is expanded extensionally. It turns out that both establishing reference and making expressions or sentences are made by connecting (or assigning) the distinct to the distinct.

The notion of the grammatical connection is far from being strict. The distinct terms may be grammatically connected only for the reason that they all (and only they, no other entities) belong to language. In other words, terms A B C D, etc. are distinct and designate various objects, entities, attributes, relations, etc.... – all and only what can be expressed in language. Sentences consist of terms and terms designate sentences – a sentence constructed of the terms KNL may be designated as A, a sentence constructed of the terms FG may be designated as B, the sentence "the moon is directly between the sun and the earth" is designated as "eclipse" etc. If we gather all the terms or all the sentences – which is the same as regards our concept, for if there is the sentence KNL and, say, GHL, L of KNL and L of GHL are by no means the same – then we may regard them to be *grammatically connected as* they are all of language.

Suppose, for better perspicuity, we write down all the terms in distinct signs (all superfluous "L's" are indexed or replaced by something different or stratified and so on). Now insofar as we say that designation is of the same nature as the grammatical connection and having abstracted from the fact that the distinct terms are to designate something (or at least most of them), can we say there is certain "designation" concerning terms themselves? Can there be some "irregular" designation between each of the terms?

In the case of usual expressions, where terms designate objects – such as NKL, "the sun rises every day", etc. – the requirement that terms within expressions should *designate* each other may sound absurd. But if the grammatical connection is understood wide enough, so that terms to be connected are to be such only for the reason they appertain to language, then it is not important in which way all the terms are to be designated as names of objects. In this case, having in mind that designation – assigning of a meaning – and that the grammatical connection are based on the distinctness of terms, it would make sense to make clear the role of this *designation* – its existence follows from its common base with the grammatical connection.

Thus, suppose A B C D E.... are the distinct terms of language. Let us designate A as B, AB as C, ABC as D, ABCD as E, ABCDE as F, etc.... Successor designates the predecessor simply for the reason that it is different from the predecessor. This *designating* consists in providing another sign, as an object is "provided" with a name. Just as though we "add" sign to an object – and now there exist the object and its name – as well, we "add" B to A, C to AB, D to ABC etc.... What this notion of *designation* has taken from the designation proper is just distinctness understood as it is constrained within what is designating and what is designated.

But we still call it designation because this is the process of giving a name to names which are not (any of them) the name that is being given. If terms must be distinct, the process is what tests this. One is consecutively juxtaposed to others for the reason of being none of the others. This way some explicit order is created: if some terms (objects) are distinct i.e. identifiable as such, there must exist some order to identify them. If there were no order to verify their distinctness (distinguishing each from the others itself implies some order), it would be meaningless to tell whether they are distinct or not.

Thus, the abstract assertion that terms are distinct implies that terms are placed or situated or conceived in a definite manner, but in no matter which definite manner (no matter which distinct term may follow another).

This manner in question, having been carried out, may be fixed. We may simply choose or imagine any sign (or term), e.g. A, and place beside it another term, e.g. B, not A, then place beside them another one, not A and not B, and so on. What we yield is a model of all the terms of language, as the concept of the Grammar requires them to be. Fixing this series we may use it as names for any objects. This way some objects may be named, but this way all the objects may be named. This series is the ready-made names for all the objects, entities, attributes, relations, signs proper or whatever, intended to guarantee the fulfillment of the requirement language is burdened, i.e. the requirement of distinctness of the terms.

(Were we quite precise saying that a sign is to "replace" an object? It seems that this is not precisely so. A sign does not replace an object, it *implies* the object; the notion of a sign is not inseparable from its reference and objects are in the same sense not inseparable from words. Respectively – having in mind that to designate means, in a sense, to juxtapose different to different – e.g., F of the series "implies" ABCDEF, B "implies" AB, D "implies" ABCD (D, for instance, "implies" ABCD but not ABC, just in the way "replacement" or "designation" may be literally understood). But we could talk literally of *replacement* in the sense above if we set ahead the *dumb* sign 0).

These haphazardly selected or made up but orderly placed signs may be applied (as names-giving) to any objects. We needn't do anything to distinguish the objects one from another. We need not know their properties or characteristics; we need not learn or make up their names. It does not matter whether they are explicitly distinguishable, or their similarity is hard to do away with. In any case the orderly series of distinct names dubbing objects is quite able to fulfill the requirement of distinctness. To give names this way is to abstract from any properties of objects, making them remain just "objects".

And what information can we have if we know nothing about objects except that they are objects? Assigning to objects of various groups the distinct signs of the series, therefore distinguishing the objects, we yield – and this is all we can yield – ABCDEF, ABCDE, ABCD, ABC, AB, A and the like, for each of those groups; or abbreviating, respectively, F, E, D, C, B, A. (Note that the groups (namely the groups of objects), as merely objects, are not distinguished in any way.) These are the signs of the series which determine which groups there are and what is a group – to group is to characterize, and lack of characteristics proper allows no other way to do. Thus, each object of the corresponding group may be named as A, B, C, D, E in the corresponding order; and each object of another group may be named as A, B; and each object of the according group as A, B, C; etc.... And each of the groups themselves must be named, respectively, E, B and C; for to distinguish a group we must have as names E, B, C, but not as any other names of objects in any of those groups.

Distinguishing or testing the distinctness of each term from others necessarily requires succession, no matter whether in place or in time. To be in the succession means to have been checked as distinct. Since in the succession the requirement of distinctness is satisfied, those may be any terms (a definite place in the succession may be occupied by no matter which term different from the others) and they may mean anything (since the requirement is satisfied, no matter what they are to denote). Any haphazardly taken terms in any such succession may mean anything. Thus, any usual sentence may have a meaning which has nothing in common with what it is ordinarily considered to mean. At first glance it may seem absurd, but actually codes are based on that.

May there be another word for each of the terms to be different from the others? How can be called each term if it is called "term" only because it is single, distinct from others of this very kind? The answer is easy to suggest: this is a "unit". Whatever a sign may mean – it may mean even some units, actually; as a *sign* which can be only different from all others, it may be only a unit.

If something (A) is iterated (AA) and that (A) together with the other which is "iterating" that (A), i.e. (AA), must by no means be deemed that (A),(i.e. (A) must not be deemed (AA)), and what is "iterating" that (A), i.e. (– A) is by no means that (A); then both that (A) and what is "iterating" that (A), i.e.(– A), are units, but are by no means the same unit, i.e. (A) is not (– A); and as units, neither (A), nor (– A) may be (AA).

On the other hand, (AA) may be designated as no A, e.g. (B), and may be called a "unit", as well as both A and the other A, but all of them are not one and the same unit. The notion of unit is adequate to the distinctness of a term as regards to other terms. Note that the distinct terms of language are adequate to "unit" independently of their meaning. "Half" is a unit, but a half is not. "Infinity" is a unit, but infinity is not a unit. The notion of unit comes out of distinctness; other arithmetical notions are derived from that of unit.

Since all the terms A; B; C; D; are distinct, those terms in their succession ABCD.... differ each from the next in the succession exactly by unit. To increase by unit means to test distinctness of a term as regards all the others previously so tested.

A sign, once uttered or written may be regarded as an object. As such, it may be named – the name differs from a sign – then those two signs may be named by some sign, different from each of them, and so on. Or, which is the same in our case; we may connect one sign to another. In each of the cases (connecting or designating) we are checking each new one to be distinct from each of the others. It is absolutely unimportant which signs are used, only their definite places in succession matter. Thus, one may use terms as "my cat Felix", "the Queen of England", "the boots I've worn for three years" etc., in a given succession. If he has poor imagination or no other favorite things, he may compose other terms out of those three terms and give them proper places further in the single succession. Applying those terms in this succession as names of various kinds of objects, he yields not multifarious but very definite information that this amount of objects has the places of the succession up to "the Queen...." and that amount of objects has the places up to "the boots....". If the terms of the succession (these ones or ABCD.... or any) are conventionally fixed – not only any terms are definitely placed in the succession, but conventionally definite terms are definitely placed, then we yield the natural numbers.

In a sense, as the terms of language are distinct, the natural numbers are the testing of their distinctness. The succession may be constructed (or be tried to be constructed at its beginning) out of all known terms (say, items of the dictionary) or it may be constructed out of some special terms – the subject applies the members of the succession (the natural numbers) to all the objects, since the requirement of distinctness is fulfilled therefore. Applying the natural numbers, we are fulfilling the requirement, e.g. assigning numerals to similar things or terms. The way assumption runs is that terms are distinct, implying that they are distinct even if they cannot be distinguished by the subject. The subject checks the distinctness of some *fixed* terms to apply them to similar objects to distinguish them one from another or applying them to similar terms, therefore making them distinct. Thus, the natural numbers appear to be a device of the subject to make similar terms distinguishable or – which is the same, if the terms in question are, say, "object", "object".... – to discern different objects or entities. This is a device that allows different looks for what should have different meanings.

According to those simple speculations, the natural numbers do not look as something elementary, intrinsic to nature itself along with other elementary things like language. Rather the notion of the natural numbers looks like that dependent on the notion of the Grammar of language – they are just a device that helps to keep in sight the characteristic property of language.

Each term of the succession is the successor to the previous only because it is distinct from all the previous. It cannot be a member of the succession only because it is a successor, for the succession is built on the basis of distinctness. Any term may serve as the beginner of the succession. A term may be composed of other terms and iterated terms give others; hence, evidently, there can be no term which ends the distinct terms. To say that the beginner is equal to any of its successors means to say that they are not distinct, which is impossible. In the fixed succession (succession with definite terms) the terms are chosen arbitrary; if some of them are to be replaced by another, the one which is replacing must be tested anew as regards its distinctness to the others, in particular to the predecessor.

Suppose we have a term. It may be any term. It may be some quite occasional one like "the boots...." It may serve as a beginner of a succession. As a term of language it has the property of distinctness. Suppose that having begun from that term, we have tested some terms to be distinct from each other, making a succession. All those terms have the property of distinctness. If we took some other term and check its distinctness from all those terms, then it follows, naturally, that we established its distinctness, too. But then, it follows that this is the property which all the terms of the succession we are constructing should have.

It seems that the above paragraphs are able to convince that Peano axioms (in the previous paragraph we mean the principle of induction) may be expressed in terms of the Grammar, therefore introducing the notion of the natural numbers. Peano axioms are suitable to be a basis of a formal theory but they could hardly explain counting explicitly (though, evidently, *implicitly* they provide the series to consist of the distinct terms, (successors)).

As for the concept of the Grammar, the natural numbers are the conventionally universal names, tested to be distinct, which can be applied for all the objects. The order is how they are tested each regarding all the others. Any names may be tested whether they are distinct, each to each, providing the single series. Any breaking of the order would not be justified. Thus, if we have got the tested series ABCD, we could not say that it might be as well ACBD, for we should have called another reason, other than just to be distinct, for CD to be DC (or to be either CD or DC) there should have been stipulated some property, characteristic or an operation over the operation of distinguishing of those terms. The natural numbers are the very names that have already been tested in such a way. It is intuitively clear that to assign those names in the order they are means to count. (Those naming guarantees the difference of the terms).

Literally Peano axioms are: there is the initial number, for any natural number there is a successor, no successor is equal to the initial number, if two successors are equal then their predecessors are equal; induction: suppose the initial number has some property and, for any number if from the fact that a number has the property follows that its successor has this property, then all the numbers have this property. We may suppose that the axiom that if two successors are equal, then their predecessors are equal implies distinctness of the successors (together with the initial number). But this hardly gives an intuitive notion of counting. Applying directly the axioms to the objects to be counted we yield "....successor, successor of the successor, successor of the successor of the successor....."

This is not reminiscent of counting. Rather this may remind us of the concept of number propounded by Frege and Neumann. They say that a number is the class of classes. Thus, there are two cats, two sets, etc.; and then "two" is the class of all classes with the property "two". But the resemblance to the concept of the Grammar seems to be in the iteration. The class of classes of two objects is no class of any objects with the property "two" – "two" is something different than a class, this is the class of classes. This is how the concept should sound in our interpretation. "Successor of the successor" is something that is still to be named in order not to be taken for "successor"; and hence in order to *count*, but not to multiply what is to be counted, i.e. the same entities.

We grammatically connect distinct terms – we connect A to B and C to B (or to AB) – because we cannot connect A to A or B to B, if we do we yield, respectively, AC and BD or Q and P (AA is AC or Q, but not A; and BB is BD or P, but not B). The Grammar says that the iterated term is no that term (not the initial). It is this restriction that makes terms distinct. When we write down terms which look distinct: A, B; we are showing that the terms A, A would not have the same meaning. In particular, that A and A have not one and the same meaning (or simply AA is not A) is that which is behind the concept of the natural numbers.

In the last section we have justified the concept of the Grammar by arithmetic – actually we asserted that the negation of the concept leads to a certain constraint in the application of addition – addition in general sense, as something is added to something, not in the strict arithmetical sense. But this was rather an appeal to common sense. Now we have justified arithmetic by the Grammar of language. Simply, the Grammar is the assertion that another similar sign must be considered as another sign, but not the same, just as another object is considered as another object, not as one and the same (and hence the sign must have another meaning within the grammatical connection the signs are). But then it is obvious that the concept of Grammar is a general concept. Naturally, the concept of the Grammar of language concerns all there are in language. And general phenomena, such as the number, must be explained directly by the concept. Rather this is what is to be expected than wondered about.

Iterations in Formal Arithmetic

If the concept of Grammar has turned out to be so general that it can serve as a basis to explain the notion of natural numbers, can there be any other basis for arithmetic, free from any need to refer to this concept in elucidating or construing its ideas? Can a concept of arithmetic be constructed that is totally independent of the Grammar of language? Or, at least, is that so with the well-known basis of arithmetic - the one which uses Peano axioms, viz. formal arithmetic?

Formal arithmetic should have been a part of Hilbert's program, conceived to prevent paradoxes in mathematics. Classical mathematics should have been formulated as formal axiomatic theory. Then its consistency (or absence of contradictions in it) should have been proved, i.e. it should have been proved that a contradiction could not be proved in this formal theory. In other words, a proof should have been found that two contradictory theorems could not be deduced from the axioms of the theory. All that was not realized and the reason of the failure lies in Goedel's result (1930, 1931), i.e. in the theorem that says that the theory cannot be both consistent and complete. It cannot be so that for any formula of the theory there is either the proof of its truth or the proof of its falsehood and at the same time there is no formula (or some) in the theory that has both the proof of its truth and the proof of its falsehood.

Roughly, the theorem says that if formal arithmetic is consistent (containing no propositions proved to be contradictory to each other), then the proof of its consistency cannot be yielded by means of formal arithmetic, i.e. any proof of this kind must apply ideas or methods which cannot be expressed in formal arithmetic.

To come to this conclusion one should firstly yield the so-called undecidable proposition, i.e. a formula that expresses its own unprovability. In standard interpretation – that is, in the interpretation where the model for the formal statements on arithmetic is arithmetic itself – Goedel's theorem states that neither this proposition nor its negation can be proved in formal arithmetic, if this arithmetic is consistent. Suppose we construct by means of formal arithmetic a formula that in accordance with standard interpretation expresses the impossibility of the proof of some formula together with its negation. This formula would be the assertion of consistency of formal arithmetic. The theorem says that if the theory is consistent, then it contains an undecidable proposition (i.e. the one of which we say that neither itself nor its negation can be proved). But if the undecidable proposition is that which cannot be proved or disproved, i.e. is unprovable, then the formula asserting the consistency is also unprovable in the theory. For this is an implication: the assertion of consistency implies an undecidable proposition; and if the proposition fails to be among the theorems of the theory – i.e. formulas of the theory whose proofs there are in the theory – nor among their negations, then the assertion also fails to be, as antecedent.

We see that the impossibility to infer the assertion of consistency of formal arithmetic – and hence, as it was conceived by Hilbert, classical mathematics in general – by means of the formal theory itself is pivoting on the discovery of undecidable propositions.

Formal arithmetic is a calculus in which recursive functions are largely applied and among whose axioms there are Peano axioms. All the symbols of the theory and expressions consisting of them are supplied with numerals (Goedel's numbers) in the mode of one-to-one correspondence: each symbol or expression corresponds to a natural number and there is a function to determine any natural number as whether corresponding to a symbol or expression, or not. This way we may substitute any statement of the formal system by the equivalent statement in the natural numbers, then expressing those natural numbers in terms of the formal system, i.e. as according symbols of the system (for the natural numbers and operations on them are namely what is to be expressed in symbols of formal arithmetic).

Goedel's numbers is a code whose members are some natural numbers for the symbols, but the numbers themselves have their own symbols in the system.

We may equivalently make statements in symbols of formal arithmetic and in Goedel's numbers (in a code whose symbols are natural numbers).

Suppose we have a function or relation in symbols of formal arithmetic. This expression has a free variable – that which is not quantified. Let us take Goedel's number of this expression in symbols of formal arithmetic as the value of this variable. The expression constructed this way has its own Goedel's number. It is proved in formal arithmetic that such constructions may be represented as formulas of the theory in its symbols. Thus, there is a function whose argument is Goedel's number of any formula of the system with a free variable and whose value is Goedel's number of the formula yielded by the former one by replacing the variable with the symbol of its Goedel's number. There is a relation whose formula contains an argument which is Goedel's number of a formula with a free variable and the other argument is Goedel's number of the proof of the latter formula with the symbol of its Goedel's number instead of the variable.

We choose this ridiculous way to expose formulas of a formal system in order to display the iterations which those formal constructions contain.

Each formula of formal arithmetic correlates to its Goedel's number. Any expression of a formula may be replaced by the expression of the corresponding Goedel's number. To name a Goedel's number means to name a formula. But the theory also allows construction of formulas which are made by formulas and these formulas own Goedel's numbers. To correlate Goedel's numbers to these constructions we should consider Goedel's numbers of formulas of which they are made. We may say that Gödel's numbers of these constructions are no Goedel's numbers; they are Goedel's numbers of Goedel's numbers. Keeping in mind the nature of Goedel's numbers, we may also say that the constructions are formulas of formulas within the formal theory.

Undecidable propositions belong to this kind of constructions. Above we have described in words the relation which may be expressed in formal arithmetic as its formula: Rel(u,y), where u is Goedel's number of some formula A(x) – x is a free variable – and y is Goedel's number of the proof of the formula A(u), where u denotes the Goedel's number u as a sign of formal arithmetic. Suppose Rel(x, y) is the formula denoting this relation in formal arithmetic. Suppose the formula Gen(y) NegRel(x, y) will play the role of A(x) in the definition of the relation. Then, if m is the sign denoting Goedel's number of Gen(y)NegRel(x, y) in formal arithmetic notation, we replace: Gen(y)NegRel(m, y). The formula Gen(y) NegRel (m, y) is an undecidable proposition of formal arithmetic. It represents the Goedel's number of the Goedel's number of the formula Gen(y) NegRel(x, y). If we supposed n to be the Goedel's number of the proof of the formula Gen(y)NegRel(m, y) – given in the notation of formal arithmetic, then by means of the theory we would deduce two contradictory formulas from the formula Gen(y)NegRel(m, y).

It is clear that any description of the procedure with whose help the undecidable proposition has been generated may be paraphrased as making Goedel's number of the Goedel's number of a formula (or, e.g. a proposition of a proposition). The formal theory does not explicitly consider iterations in its basis – namely in Peano axioms, and neither anywhere else – but nevertheless they appear in it – constructions founded on iterations are proved to be expressible in the theory, generating propositions of the theory whose truth or falsehood cannot be proved by its own means. Avoiding determining iterations explicitly the formal theory – an extension of ordinary language – the theorists have to reveal them in another way and recognize their role – the determination of their truth or falsehood must be beyond the theory that does not consider them in its basis. There is a known example of this beside the undecidable proposition. Tarski's result, where, roughly, the notion of arithmetical truth is not arithmetically determined, is reached by applying, in the according theorem, a construction, similar to the above mentioned.

As it is with ordinary language, formal theories in certain contexts are regarded as paradoxical – and this is due to the case with undecidable propositions. Asserting their own unprovability, the propositions are found to be analogous even to semantical paradoxes (Wang Hao 1962).

Thus, a conception of arithmetic can be constructed without explicitly determining iterations – unlike it is done in the concept of Grammar – but it does not mean that iterations would not be expressible in this conception and this conception would not be able to generate propositions of the arithmetic which could not be regarded as containing iterations.

Numbers by Convention

We can keep within the requirement of the Grammar of language – i.e. within the requirement of distinctness of the terms of language – putting down a sign which is distinct from the previous one: A; B....; not allowing a sign to be repeated. But we also are keeping within the requirement when we repeat a sign, for repetition in accordance with the requirement should involve the *appearing* of another sign, distinct from the repeated: A A generate B. This provides for all the signs that they are distinct from each other, for having A A B, we can make of the repeated A (the second A) and of B a term distinct from A and from B. That is, writing the composed term in column:

    B
A A B

    B

Regarding A A B as a term and having in mind that repetition should generate a term different from that which has been repeated, we yield:

    B   B

A A B A A B C

Any term of this series must be different from another; any of them must consist of different terms than any other. Again, the composed terms are written in columns:

```
              C
    B     C  B  C
A A B  A  A  B  C
```

Again, let us regard the expression above as a whole, i.e. as a term. Let us agree that in order to satisfy the requirement of distinctness one should repeat a term to yield another term different from the given and the repeated ones – in previous sections we were satisfying the requirement not repeating terms. Thus, we yield:

```
                     D
     C          D D D C
  B  C B C   B C C B D D D
A A B A A B C A A B A A B C D
```

We may continue this way putting after two similar terms one different from them and this will suffice to make all the terms distinct. We are intuitively sure that the procedure, according to which we are to repeat a sign (or a term) and put another sign, provides precisely as many signs to join to the same signs to make composed signs be different one from another as it is necessary for the aim of making all the same signs in the series be different. In other words, we *believe* that the procedure allows us to turn the same signs resulting in it into the same number of sets, while we are joining properly different signs to those same signs. Thus, when the procedure runs:

A A B A A B C....

we shouldn't have more, not less signs but, exactly the same number of them which allows us to construct the series of different sets:

```
            C
      B   C B C
A A B A A B C ....
```

Ultimately the procedure gives the same result as the connection of the distinct terms does, i.e. the distinct terms. Those distinct terms are represented precisely by subsets of the set of the distinct terms which are generated by repetitions of the terms in the procedure (the generated terms are italicized: *A* A *B* A A *B C*). This must be the single procedure, for there cannot be any other members of the sets (A), (A.B), (B), (A, C), (A, B, C), (B, C), (C), (A, B, D), etc., each of which is taken from one of the sets and from each of the sets only one member is taken (A A B A A B C, etc.).

Now suppose that to be distinct from any other means to be just in another position (say, on paper). That is, a sign may look absolutely identical to another one, but it occupies a different position, e.g. A A, or any.

The same signs are often implied distinct as regards to their position in mathematics, e.g. 0, 999.... On the other hand, there are definitions of a set which runs that a set is a collection of objects which are not necessarily distinct, so a set may be represented as, e.g. (A, B, A, C, D, C, A....). But in accordance with our assumption we will adhere to the view that even if the same sign designates once more the same object, this will be *another* designation of the object. Language has means to express identity, but this has to be expressed with different signs. Suppose the concept of Grammar is that which requires marking the same sign by another to distinguish it, but another position may be regarded as that which substitutes the "mark" satisfactory. In particular, there is nothing to prevent regarding the ordered pair (x, x) in this general sense.

The characteristic property of ordered pairs – (x, y), or ordered n-tuples (x, y, z...u_n), is that (x, y) is equal to (v, u) if and only if x is equal to v and y is equal to u. An ordered pair – it may always be generalized to an ordered n-tuple – is defined as (x, y) = ((x), (x, y)). The assertion that if (x, y) = (v, u), then x = v and y = u is known as Kuratowski's theorem. Its proof is based on the definition of an ordered pair (x, y) as ((x), (x, y)) and on the notion of inclusion (e.g. (x) is included in ((x), (x, y))). The definition is done purposely to prove this theorem, i.e. (x, y) = ((x), (x, y)) is simply a technical device to yield the assertion that if (x, y) = (v, u), then x = v and y = u.

Obviously we would be in the right to assert that the inclusion applied in the proof, as well as brackets – in the proof two types of brackets are usually applied, those for (x, y) and those for ((x), (x, y)) – are nothing but technical devices to demonstrate that if the expression x y is understood as x x y, then (if in the expression both x and y are substituted respectively for any signs) the order of x y, or what they are substituted for, must be respectively preserved: y, or what it is substituted for, must follow x, or what it is substituted for. If x y is x x y; then for any x, y, u and v; if x y is u v then x is u and y is v.

A member of an ordered pair (or n-tuple) is identified as such if and only if its position in the pair is determined. A member may be any – x may be substituted for u or for anything – but the position should be the same – x or anything it may be substituted for should be at the place where it is in the ordered pair (x, y). We may say that difference in the position entirely characterizes members of n-tuples. Each member differs from another, for it occupies a different place. Since it was stipulated that position indicates distinctness, we conclude that we actually come to the notion of numbers as based on the concept of the Grammar. If we exclude the possibility of appearing the same signs in n-tuples – (x, x) – we are in the right to say that members of n-tuples are numbers.

Thus, excluding expressions as (x, x), or accepting that another position in an n-tuple guarantees another signs for all the signs, we may say that according to the result of Kuratowski's theorem the expression x x y implies that y follows x for any x and y, to put it roughly; and so x x y determines the notion of numbers as it is understood in accordance with the concept of the Grammar. In other words, applying the result of the theorem, we may easily conclude that the principle that iteration of a sign generates another sign – x x y is simply a record of this – has the natural numbers as its consequence.

We have said that the natural numbers are the result of the property of distinctness and a convention. Any terms may be tested as distinct: A B C D..., or others. This is the matter of convention to determine which tested terms (signs) are to be applied as the numbers. Now we know that this conventionality itself is not of an arbitrary character but is conceptually backed. It is possible to chose the single series of signs if it is the case that whatever we take as a tested series, we are to consider them equal since they are to designate any objects: (A B C ....)=(L M N....)=(....).... ; but according to the Kuratowski's theorem A=L=.... ,B=M=.... ,C=N=.... ,....

Thus, if we take the principle, which is tantamount to the assumption of distinctness, that A A generates anything but not A, we can regard the natural numbers as a particular case of ordered n-tuples (the case where even if members of n-tuples are the same, they must be considered to differ by virtue of their position in an n-tuple; or, to put it in other way, if we restrict ordered n-tuples only to the case where their members are different). This allows making the conclusion that the main property of ordered n-tuples gives the *possibility* to reduce any number of the possible series of the tested distinct terms to the one series which can be established by a convention.

The Continuum Hypothesis

The principle "an iteration of a sign generates another sign" is thus another way of asserting the assumption of the distinctness of terms of language. The necessity of the record x x y implies that x x may be either substituted for y or the iterated x may be cancelled and substituted for y or y may be joined
$$y$$
to an x, making another sign x x y – each alternative satisfies the requirement of distinctness and is at the discretion of the subject.

This principle (or rule) is applied when no special meaning is meant. This principle is to be followed when we need not be bothered with marking an iterated sign to show that it must have an altered meaning or give distinct names to objects which are otherwise indistinguishable. And a lack of objects does not imply a lack of counting, rather counting runs within the creation of new signs: so to say, iterations themselves are counted. That is, A, B, C... are numbers, each term is in brackets and created numbers are italicized:

$$(((((A)(A)B)((A)(A)B))C)(((A)B)((A)(A)B))C)))D....$$

As it was said, this generates the distinct terms represented by a set (it contains the italicized signs as members) and its proper subsets in columns:

```
              C
       B    C B C
   A A B A  A B C ....D ....
```

Iterations generate distinct signs to be joined to the iterated signs to make them distinct.

Let us omit members of subsets over the iterations and count all the subsets using traditional number-signs: 1, 2, 3....n, and adding the zero-sign:

(There were cultures, though, which invented and successfully applied arithmetic without a zero-sign).

1 2 3 4 5 6 7 8 9 10 11 12 13 14 15 16 n
O A A B A A B C A A B A A B C D....n.

Or, using powers of 2, we yield:

2^1 2^2 2^3 2^4 2^n

O A A B A A B C A A B A A B C D.... n....

Or, applying for clarity traditional notation overall:

2^1 2^2 2^3 2^4 2^n
0 1 1 2 1 1 2 3 1 1 2 1 1 2 3 4.... n....

We see that 1 1 generates 2, 1 1 2 1 1 2 generates 3 and so on; to yield the number n there must be 2^n subsets, not more and not less. Suppose N denotes the infinity of all the natural numbers. Suppose the cardinal of the infinity of the natural numbers is N_0 (aleph 0). Let us designate the cardinal which is the next one bigger to N_0 as N_1 (aleph 1). For N to be generated there must be not more and not less than 2^N subsets (or 2^N numbers together with the iterations to generate them). Then the cardinal N_1, the next to

the cardinal N_0, must be equal to 2^{N_0} ($N_1 = 2^{N_0}$).

(A series of bigger cardinals *generates* a series of fewer cardinals, for numbers are generated by iterations).

The assertion $N_1 = 2^{N_0}$ is called the Continuum Hypothesis.

Sets:

The Continuum Hypothesis 39

$$
\begin{array}{l}
C \\
BC\ B\ C \\
O\ A\ A\ B\ A\ A\ B\ C\ ....D....
\end{array}
\qquad (*)
$$

are distinct. Thus, each of them may be generated by iteration of a sign (or term) which is different from the set (from the sign or signs the set is designated). For instance (the members of the sets above the iterated members are omitted and the distinct sets are in brackets; not in columns):

$$2^4$$

OX X (A) X X (A) (AB) X X (A) X X (A) (AB) (B)....(**)

We can continue this way:

$$2^4$$

OY Y (X) Y Y (X) (XA) Y Y (X) Y Y (X) (XA) (A).... (***)

$$2^4$$

O Z Z (Y) Z Z (Y) (YX) Z Z (Y) Z Z (Y) (YX) (X)....(****)

....

....

....

Thus, if there are sets, there is continuum.

It is clear that if O A B C D .... has the cardinal N_0, then (*) has the cardinal $N_1 = 2^{N_0}$. If (*) has the cardinal N_1, then (**) has the cardinal $N_2 = 2^{N_1}$. If (**) has the cardinal N_2, then (***) must have the cardinal $N_3 = 2^{N_2}$. And if (***) has the cardinal N_3, then (****) has the cardinal $N_4 = 2^{N_3}$. And so on, for A B C D... is generated by A iteration, A A B iteration etc. in (*); (*) is generated by X iteration, X X A iteration etc. in (**); (**) is generated by Y iteration, Y Y X iteration, etc. in (***); (***) is generated by Z iteration, Z Z Y iteration, etc. in (****); and so on.

In general, for any x, the cardinal $N_{x+1}=2^{N_x}$, i.e. each further cardinal is equal to the number of subsets of its predecessor. This assertion is called the Generalized Continuum Hypothesis.

Both assertions, the Continuum Hypothesis and the Generalized Continuum Hypothesis, were deduced from the principle that iteration of a sign generates another sign, or directly from the mode sets are to be generated according to the principle.

Thus, the concept of Grammar has the Continuum Hypothesis as its consequence. But this is not the case with formal theories. While the Continuum Hypothesis and the Generalized Continuum Hypothesis are immediately deduced from the fashion sets are to be constructed as it is required by the concept of the Grammar, the Continuum Hypothesis is proved to be independent of the axioms of set theories. (Moreover, it has been proved (Goedel 1938, 1940) that the assertion of the Generalized Continuum Hypothesis implies the assertion of the axiom of choice. This axiom is based on no other principle than forming a set by taking a member from a set – without any special characteristics of the members. This indeterminacy of characteristics raised objections.) The independency made clear that it could not be justified by other axioms – if the theory has no contradictions, it won't have them if the Hypothesis is added. It was proved that the Continuum Hypothesis could not be disproved within the axioms and it was proved that its negation added to the other axioms yielded no contradictions – Goedel (1939) ruled out a disproof of the Continuum Hypothesis and Cohen's work (1966) ruled out a proof of the Continuum Hypothesis. That is, neither a positive nor a negative solution can be given. And the statements that cannot be proved or disproved are called "undecidable propositions" – Cohen called the Continuum Hypothesis "a very dramatic example" of undecidable propositions (1966 p.1).

Above we have regarded the undecidable propositions arisen in formal arithmetic. Those propositions were generated by iterations, i.e. as a matter of fact they were Goedel's numbers of Goedel's numbers – this kind of constructions could be neither proved nor disproved. And we see that the assertion which is called the Continuum Hypothesis arises from the notion of sets formation given by the Grammar, i.e. from the assertion that an iteration of a sign generates another sign. Meanwhile neither of the formal theories – formal arithmetic and set theory – has the explicit assertion to be introduced into the axioms or some basic principles which may be construed as tantamount to what Grammar says. It seems that being extensions of natural language, the formal theories are able to form propositions generated by iterations but are not able to decide their falsehood or truth because of the lack of according postulates.

Generally, it must be remembered that, the formal theories were intended to get rid of paradoxes in mathematical statements. These were logical paradoxes, i.e. the assertions formed by iterations whose truth or falsehood – if you do not consider or do not recognize the real Grammar of natural language – cannot be decided in language. Undecidable propositions of formal theories are formed by iterations and their falsehood or truth cannot be proved by means of the theories. This way the formal theories – extensions of natural language – oust what they are intended to avoid.

The Rich Man's Argument

The thesis that grammatically connected terms of language must be different – or the thesis that terms alter their meaning within any grammatical connection, no matter whether they are the same or not – is not just a device purposed to construe problems concerning formal theories or foundations of arithmetic. Rather this is a genuine concept on the characteristic property of ordinary language. This would be more convincing if we regarded semantical paradoxes, the ones which do not concern set theory proper.

As for logical paradoxes, we applied "the rich man's argument"; the response of the person who lives on the interest on interest and by that reason is able to distinguish "set" and "set of sets". At first glance the argument seems to be not applicable to semantical paradoxes, for one cannot see in them explicit iterations. The iterations are not really laid bare, but it does not mean they are not available.

Semantical paradoxes seem various, but actually they are constructed in one and the same mode. It does not really take much effort to reveal iterations in them. The iterations are to be there as regards the content, though they are omitted. And there is nothing artificially looking in this omission. It seems that this is just not a custom, no habit, to take just two for two and one just for one in what concerns words.

Russell's famous paradox (1919) which was firstly exposed in the same letter to Frege as "the set of all sets which are not members of themselves":

In a certain village there is a man who is a barber. This barber shaves all and only those men in the village who do not shave themselves. Query: Does the barber shave himself? Any man in the village is shaved by the barber if and only if he is not shaved by himself. Therefore in particular the barber shaves himself if and only if he does not.

The barber is the one who shaves all and only those men in the village who do not shave themselves. If he is a barber, he is the barber for those men. If he shaves himself, he is a barber for the barber. So as a barber he shaves the men who do not shave themselves, but as a barber for the barber he shaves himself.

"The barber for the barber" is not a barber, for "a barber" can be only "a barber", and "a barber for a barber" can be nothing but "a barber for a barber". As well as interest on interest cannot be just interest, not simply by the reason that it is stipulated in another item or calculated in a different way, but even if it is stipulated in the same item or calculated in similar way. As well, a finger and a finger is not a finger. The man who shaves all the men but himself and yet himself can be only a barber in the sense that he shaves all but himself and a barber of the barber in the sense that he shaves himself.

Grelling's paradox (see, e.g. Fraenkel & Barr-Hillel 1958):

The adjective "English" is English, the adjective "adjectival" is adjectival, and the adjective "polysyllabic" is polysyllabic. Each of them is autological. Others are not, thus "German" is not German adjective and "monosyllabic" is not monosyllabic. "Is the adjective "heterological" autological or a heterological one? If we decide that "heterological" is autological, then the adjective is true to itself (autological). But that makes it heterological rather than autological. If we therefore decide that the adjective "heterological" is heterological, then it is true to itself and that makes it autological.

Adjectives are words which add information about nouns or pronouns. Unlike "German", "English", "monosyllabic", "polysyllabic", etc., the words "autological" and "heterological" are defined as notions concerning adjectives, and they are in this sense adjectives of adjectives. It is by means of introducing these adjectives of adjectives – the "adjectives" which designate only the properties of adjectives – that all the adjectives are devided into those which are "true to themselves" and those which are "false to themselves". The adjective of adjective "heterological" can be neither heterological nor autological adjective – simply because this is not an adjective. Of cause it is trivially "heterological", not the opposite, but as the adjective of adjectives (those which are not true to themselves) is. Thus, it is true to itself but not like adjectives may or may not be. It is true to itself as adjectives of adjectives can be, i.e. "heterological" is heterological (and "autological" is autological).

The most ancient paradox, the Liar, has several versions. Here is one of them:

Somebody says: "I'm lying". Is he lying or telling the truth? If he is lying, he is telling the truth, for he recognizes his lie. And if he is telling the truth, he is lying, for what he is saying is a lie.

The following response would be within the line of our thesis that an iterated expression should differ from what the expression itself is:
"I say "I'm lying ". If I'm lying that "I'm lying", then I'm telling the truth, recognizing the lie – I'm lying that "I'm lying" must differ from "I'm lying". And if I'm telling the truth that "I'm lying", then I'm really lying; for what I reassert is the lie". This shows that in the formulation of the paradox that follows the utterance, the utterance itself has been obviously skipped – no one can genuinely or literally say "if he is lying, he is telling the truth...."And this shows that negation or, on the other hand, reaffirming of negation doesn't lead to contradiction – this can be only two different assertions, in one of which an expression is iterated.

The following paradox, invented by Tarski (1956), is usually regarded, as well as many others, as a version of the Liar, but actually it contains another iterated expression:

c is a typographical abbreviation of the expression "the sentence printed on the 3-rd line from above". Consider now the following sentence
c is not a true sentence
Having regarded to the meaning of the symbol "c", we can establish empirically:

a) "c is not a true sentence" is identical with c

Any sentence in quotation marks is considered to be true if and only if it is adequate to the fact it describes, e.g. "it is snowing" is a true sentence if and only if it is snowing. Thus,

b) "c is not true sentence" is a true sentence if and only if c is not a true sentence.

The premises a) and b) together at once give a contradiction: c is a true sentence if and only if c is not a true sentence.

The sentence a) is simply not correct. No matter in which sophisticated way it might be stated, "c is not true sentence" cannot be identical with c; and it is not stipulated straightforward that belonging to the 3-rd line renders it contradictory. The sentence "c is not a true sentence", obviously – if at all it can be identical to any sentence except itself – can be identical only to "the sentence on the sentence c". With this expression the conclusive statement of the paradox should have been the following: "the sentence on the sentence c is a true sentence if and only if c is not a true sentence". (The sentence on the sentence in question is "c is not a true sentence". Putting the latter phrase in the quotation marks on the place of "the sentence on the sentence c" in our conclusive statement, we simply yield b)).

Richard's paradox:

Let us consider all those real numbers between 0 and 1 that can be uniquely characterized by sequences of English words of any finite but un bounded length e.g. " point eight", "the positive square root of point zero seven four", "the smallest number satisfying the condition that the sum of the square of this number and its product by point one equals point three".

Clearly, there are only denumerably many of such numbers. Let us R be their set. R can be then enumerated. Consider any such enumeration. We now characterize a real number r as "that real number between 0 and 1 whose n-th digit after the decimal point is a cyclic sequent of the n-th digit of the n-th number in the enumeration under consideration" (where "1" is the cyclic sequent of "0"...., and "0" the cyclic sequent of "9".).

It follows that r is different from all numbers of R and is therefore not uniquely characterizable by finite sequence of English words in plain contradictions to the fact that r has just been characterized in this fashion, viz. by quotationed sequence of English words in the preceding sentence.

The quotationed (would be) characteristic of r has been yielded in no other way but with the help of a characteristic from R, somehow enumerated. Hence this is a characteristic by a characteristic. And R is a set of characteristics in sequences of English words, not a set of characteristics by characteristics (the latter, though, also can be expressed in sequences of English words). Thus, if we compose a sequence of English words in the above said way, this is a characteristic; but if we compose a sequence using the sequence that has been composed (say, in the way it has been done in the paradox), then this is a characteristic by the characteristic. The latter iteration suggests that the quotationed sequence does not belong to "characteristics" at all, and then is different from any element of R and at the same time can be expressed in a sequence of English words.

This paradox, like nearly all of them, may have a number of versions (we hope that we have chosen one of the simplest versions (Fraenkel & Bar-Hillel 1958)). But instead of dwelling on them, it would make perfect sense to regard its basis. As it is often asserted in literature, this paradox is based on Cantor's diagonal method. For this reason some ascribe special significance to this paradox, for it may be regarded as a parody or a sort of caricature of the method.

Cantor used his diagonal method to prove innumerability of certain sets. Suppose there is an enumeration of functions with one variable, e.g. x. We place them in a column one below another. The rows are values of the functions, while the variables of each function are natural numbers:

$F_1(X) \; F_1(1) \; F_1(2)....$

$F_2(X) \; F_2(1) \; F_2(2)....$

....

Now we can define a "function whose values are the next natural number to the values of the functions enumerated whose numerals (numbers assigned to the rows) are equal to the values of the argument x". The function is $f(x) = f_x(x) + 1$. Obviously this function has the single variable x and stays out of the enumeration of all such functions. This function by such functions (a function that is devised with the help of this kind of functions) has its values correlated to the values of the functions along the diagonal of the thus yielded table.

The same thought may be expressed in another way.

Let us place series of the natural numbers one below another and there should be as many of the series as there are natural numbers.

1 2 3 4....
1 *2* 3 4....
1 2 *3* 4....
1 2 3 *4*....

....

Together with the series we have written we yield the superfluous series – that which is italicized. In this context the description of the series simply as "the natural numbers" could not be full – it could be full if we removed all other figures except the italicized. We may call the italicized figures "the series of the series" or "the natural numbers by all the natural numbers", for they could not arise without the series so written.

Paradoxical situations are solved by revealing iterations and pointing out their difference from the notions to be iterated, e.g. there are characteristics of natural numbers in English words and there are such characteristics yielded by using such characteristics – the latter ones exist if and only if the former do exist. But paradoxes do not necessarily arise where such iterations may appear, they arise within certain contexts.

Berry's paradox often is said to sound similar to the latter one (one of the versions seen in Quine (1969)):

There are only finitely many of English syllables: hence only finitely many natural numbers each of which is specifiable in fewer than 24 syllables; and hence "*a least natural number not specifiable in fewer than 24 syllables*". But this has been just specified in 23 syllables.

We may specify any natural number in any way in 24 syllables in case the natural number yields such a specification, but just at the very moment we introduce in our specification the word "specifiable" (or a synonym) referring to the number, we yield a specification of the specification
. The negation containing in the phrase contains in the specification of the specification, but not to just in the specification of natural numbers in English syllables.

Russell's well known paradox concerning the word "impredicable" (Fraenkel & Bar-Hillel 1958):

Some properties apply to themselves, some not. The property of being red does not apply to itself, since the property of being red is surely not red, whereas the property of being abstract, being itself abstract applies to itself. Calling the property of not applying to itself "impredicable", we arrive at the paradoxical consequence that impredicable is impredicable if and only if it is not.

To be exact, "impredicable" is the property of not applying properties. It designates a certain property of properties. When we apply it to itself, we apply the property of the properties to be not applying to themselves. But as "impredicable" is defined, it is to be applied only to properties but not to properties of properties. The paradox is anologue to Grelling's (though it concerns "properties", not "adjectives").

The Mayor (often ascribed to Kleene):

In a certain country each municipality has a mayor and two different municipalities cannot have one and the same mayor. Sometimes a mayor does not live in his own municipality. Suppose a law obliges all the mayors who do not live in their own municipalities to live in some territory S. S forms a municipality. Where should the mayor of S live? He cannot live in S, for within the law only the mayors who do not live in their own municipalities can live there. But according to the law, if he does not live in his own municipality, he should live in S.

Since he is not just a mayor, but the "mayor of the mayors" who do not live in their own municipalities, he can live in S just keeping within the law. He is something different than a mayor in a municipality.

The oldest version of the Liar is the version made up by Epimenides, the Cretan. He said that all the Cretans were liars. But being himself a Cretan was he a liar or not?

A Cretan who states that all the Cretans are liars is not just a liar, but a "liar to liars" at this moment. We cannot say that since he is a Cretan – and hence, as he states, a liar – he lies that all the Cretans are liars and for this reason is not a liar. For when he says that all the Cretans are liars – though being himself a Cretan, in this particular case he is a liar to the liars. Cretans including him are liars when talking about anything, but when he calls them liars, he is a liar to the liars, and he is just a liar as all the Cretans when saying anything.

Among a great number of versions of this paradox there is this one: "this sentence is false". After the query whether it is true or false it is concluded that it is false if and only if it is true.

We are to repeat most of the speculations we gave above about the version of the paradox that was regarded first. To decide whether the sentence "this sentence is false" is false or true; we cannot avoid forming sentences on the sentence. The two: ""this sentence is false" is false" and ""this sentence is false" is true", or of the kind. These two different sentences on the same sentence have different meanings, but it does not mean that the sentence (i.e. "this sentence is false") is true and false at the same time. We cannot conclude paradoxicality of the sentence from sentences on the sentence (they are something different than the sentence, and than any sentence), but we can conclude neither paradoxicality nor anything, not constructing sentences on the sentence. As in the case with the phrase "I'm lying", we cannot formulate a contradiction or anything else not saying something more than the phrase (or the sentence); but if we say more, we can only yield sentences on the uttered sentence which must have their own meaning (sentences on a sentence are not sentences).

Some insist that the sentence or the phrase (lying of itself) must be the singly uttered, therefore forming the sentence so that any context or interpretation should be excluded, e.g. "The only phrase I'm saying on such-and-such date at such-and-such time is false". But, as it was said, this is impossible to formulate a paradox and not to make sentences on the sentence. And if we "sentence" on the sentence that it is false if and only if it is true, we yield a sentence on the sentence that has no more and no less ground to exist as any other sentence on this sentence (of cause if we at all can consent with so plain breaking of the law of non-contradiction as that).

There are many paradoxes which actually have a sentence on a sentence as their base; that is, if there was no such notion, they could not be invented. One of the most often quoted is the following:

On a card, on one side there is "the sentence on the other side is false", on the other side, "the sentence on the other side is true". Hence each sentence is true if it is false and is false if it is true.

On one side we have the sentence which says that it is false that the sentence on this side is true. And on the other side we have the sentence which says that it is true that the sentence on this side is false. It's a sophisticated way to say that they are false if and only if they are false.

It seems easy to see that in the phrase:

>   (*)*We cannot prove the statement which is arrived at by substituting (*) for the variable in the statement form x.*

What we can really arrive at is the statement on the statement.

Likewise with the phrase:

"does not produce a true statement when appended to its own quotation" produce a true statement when appended to its own quotation. Appended to its own quotation it is: ""does not produce a true statement when appended to its own quotation" does not produce a true statement when appended to its own quotation" produces a statement on the statement in the (inner) quotations. It is no doubtly true to append it to its own quotation, but as the statement on the statement.

Let us regard the sentence:

>   *(*) if (*) is true, then it will snow tomorrow.*

>   *By modus ponens, given (*) and its antecedent, then the consequence is true. Since the antecedent of (*) is equivalent to (*), we assert (*) unconditionally. Then we have "(*) is true". By modus ponens again, we have proved: it will snow tomorrow.*

It may only be objected to this reasoning that the antecedent of (*) is not equivalent to (*). For the antecedent is (or contains) a conditional, while the whole statement, i.e. (*), is in this case a conditional of the conditional.

It is not hard to tumble to the idea that if there are paradoxes based on "sentence on sentence", then paradoxes may be devised which are based on the full chains of such sentences of sentences. They really exist. Thus, by substituting sentences on sentence to sentences (a sentence may be "sentenced" by some other sentence and may itself sentence a sentence), we may ultimately arrive at a sentence on the sentence, asserting the fallacy of a false sentence, or we may arrive at a sentence on a sentence about the sentence, which blatantly means a contradiction.

For example: (a) b is false. (b) c is false. (c) d is false. (d) a is true; or (a) b is false. (b) a and c are true. (c) a is false. If we did not realize that what asserted (a sentence) and what asserted on what was asserted (a sentence on the sentence) were to be distinct, we could believe, for instance, that a sentence ((b) of the last expression) might assert of itself to be true when it was said to be true and said to be false – actually its assertion "of itself" is the sentence on the two contradictory sentences, i.e. the sentences on the sentences (so to say, (b) of (b)'s).

Beside "sentence on sentence" and "sentence" there are a lot of confusions of the kind.

Thus, in the paradox: "A book which lists all books which do not list themselves in the bibliography", it is said of a book which lists all the books but not simply of a book. If we took it for a book, we could infer that "it lists itself if and only if it does not list itself".

And so in the paradox: "The relation between two relations when one does not have itself to the other". If we do not realize that we have met a relation of relations but not a relation (a term with another definition or meaning, another word), we could ascribe to it a property like "not having itself to the other" and keep wondering how it have itself to the other in order not to be so.

The following paradox allows us to recall paradoxes of set theory. It is often considered as a modification of Russell's paradox on the set of all sets which are not members of themselves.

A set x for which there is an infinite sequence of sets y, z, etc. (not necessary all distinct) such that . . . $<z<y<x$, ("<" is the sign of inclusion) is said to be groundless. Let K be the set of all grounded sets, i.e. all sets which are not groundless. If K is groundless, then there is a sequence y, z, etc., such that . . . $<z<y<K$. The K would be groundless as well. But $y<K$, and therefore is grounded. Therefore, K must be grounded. But then $K<K$, and we have . . . , $<K<K<K$. Hence K is also groundless".

As it is asserted in the paradox, $y<K$. Indeed, y may belong to K. but not in the very same sense as it belongs, e.g., to x. $Y<x$ as a set belongs to a set, but $y<K$ as a set belongs to a set of such-and-such sets. Thus, if we suppose that $y<K$, it does not follow that K is grounded. The set of all grounded sets may be not grounded.

As it was earlier said, a theorist must make corrections in his formal theory upon appearance of notions which are constructed in natural language with the help of iteration of a notion, giving them special definitions (different from a notion they are made of), determining their special properties.

This is one of the earliest paradoxes of set theory concerning the notion of definability: (Koenig's paradox. See Wang Hao 1962):

"The least indefinable transfinite ordinal". We may say the ordinal is defined, but as it is said in the very definition, it is "indefinable", and hence it is not defined. Thus it is defined if and only if it is not defined.

But when we utter "the least transfinite ordinal that could not be defined", we are not actually giving such a poor definition, what we are actually giving is a definition on a definition. All we are doing is judging upon the impossibility of the least transfinite ordinal's definition, or, to be precise, we are defining it as indefinable.

In similar fashion must be construed a number of paradoxes devised in one and the same way; such as "Inexpressible", "Unthinkable", "Inconceivable", "It is refutable", etc.... "Inexpressible" is nothing but an expression on the expressible, i.e. an expression on the expression, but not the expression of something that could not be expressed – which would really be very absurd. (It is constructed just by way of the grammatical connection of the sign of negation – which is expressible – and the term "expressible". Thus, we yield: expressible upon expressible). And so with the others.

It is no our task to regard all paradoxes. And it is not because the literature on paradoxes is so immense that it might be impossible to embrace all of them – the seeker would always remain unaware of some of them. All that has been said on the subject seems convincing enough to maintain that at least all the paradoxes that were in consideration are done in one and the same way. And at least all the most well known were mentioned.

It was widely recognized for a long time that paradoxes might be resolved when and only when the cause of their existence could be found. We should point out the reason of their appearance in language. It seems that the Grammar of language shows this reason: mistaking a term for another term made by iteration of the former. Once so mistaken, to the two terms one and the same meaning is ascribed, which in the context of a paradox is contradictory. In accordance with the concept of Grammar, paradoxes are an eccentric response to not having realized that generally in language repetition does not generate sameness, but it generates difference.

To know how paradoxes arise means to know how they can be made. To say that paradoxes are based on iterations is to say that to invent a paradox one should only pick up some iteration suitable for the aim (it seems, for instance, that "agenda on agenda" would be a good candidate). To bring about a contradiction, some negation should be involved in the context of iteration ("not members to themselves", "not applying to itself" etc.). (It seems that iterations like "a nihilist among nihilists" could help in making up such contexts).

This looks like for the most part a reasonable, not quite intuitive way to devise paradoxes. But it does not mean that making paradoxes can become a totally mechanical procedure, for contexts to iterations obviously require some imagination. It seems that even if this job could be reduced to an exercise, this would be an exercise that needed some resource. Thus we would leave it up to wittier minds.

This approach removes the difference between logical and semantical paradoxes, for it establishes the same basis for both. Formalism does not change the nature of language's terms.

The Laws of Logic

When we say that a term of language is distinct, we mean that once uttered, there cannot be any other such. If we say A, then we are not able to say this A again, what we can utter is another A, generally. That is, generally speaking, in language we cannot identify A and another A, a term and another term, no matter how similar they seem. Language is made so that we are to find the difference and we are able to find the difference. In language a term may be identical only to itself.

Terms denote things. And if we realize that to point at a thing is to make a sign and terms are just another sort of signs, we conclude that the only possible way to define things or to express things is to make terms (signs). Thus all we can do when we define things is to define things which are identical to themselves. Any thing is identical to itself. This is what may be said about a thing independently of whether it exists or not; whether it has physical existence, imaginary or it is just wrong. A thing is identical to itself because it is expressed in language and language consists of the distinct terms (or signs).

A distinct term can be only itself, it cannot be itself and at the same time in the same sense another term (or other terms). This A cannot be that A or B or anything except for this A. The term "unicorn" can be only this term, i.e. "unicorn"; it cannot be at the same time "not a unicorn" or "horse" or "rhinoceros" or anything together with "unicorn". "A term is distinct" means that it is distinct from others, from everything that the term is not.

Since making signs of language is the only way to express things, we may say that a thing cannot be itself and at the same time what it is not. A unicorn cannot be the unicorn and at the same time and in the same sense that which is not this unicorn, i.e. it cannot be also a cat, a horse, empty space, the "unicorn" that follows it in a grammatical connection, etc.; it can be either itself or what it is not, i.e. another animal or nothing or not that which was meant, or something that we did not even try to conceive. There is a thing and there is what it is not, but not together. A thing cannot be the thing and what it is not. It cannot contradict itself.

Distinctness of a term also implies that there are only the term and what it is distinct from. Its distinctness suggests nothing else. A term may be itself, and it may be something else but not itself; but it cannot be something that is not the term itself and not the terms which are not this term.

Thus, a thing may only be or not be and the third is not given. A unicorn may turn out to be anything but not the (or a) unicorn, but it cannot be so that it is neither unicorn nor anything but unicorn. And the same may be said about each thing without exception, thus a thing may either be or not be – the third is excluded.

As it is seen, the three laws of thought, self-identity, non-contradiction and the excluded middle may be considered as consequences of the assumption of distinctness of language's terms.

The thesis that any term is distinct strictly implies that there are only a term and what it is distinct from, but not something that represents both a term and what it is distinct from and not something that represents anything over a term and all it is distinct from. The three laws of logic make the definition of distinctness more precise. Regarding them as being so deduced from the notion of distinctness, we may say that they expose in brighter light what this notion may mean.

The three laws of logic sound as the answers to questions of a person who is very cautious in asserting something definite.

We say: "Terms of language are distinct; one term must be distinguished from another". He says: "But there are terms which are absolutely indistinguishable, identical?" – "A term must be identical only to itself". – "But then a term may not just be that term, this may be, too, what it is not?" –"A term cannot be the term and what is no this term, this would be a contradiction". – "But then there may be something that is not a term and not what the term is not?" – "The third is excluded". This sounds like the exhaustive explanation of the notion of distinctness of a term. All alternatives when it may be "blurred" – when a distinct term might be mistaken for some not very distinctive – seem to have been considered. Then, a term is not a bad thing, or at least not worse than any other – "term" may be replaced for "thing". Besides things are what terms stands for, and we are able to talk of things insofar as terms of language permit. And if they are distinct, we shall be able to talk of things in the way that follows from the distinctness of terms. Thus, anyone using language is, so to say, not deliberately cautious enough to speak of things exactly in the way they can be spoken insofar as terms of language allow.

As it is known, not all in the three laws of thought is taken by everybody as absolute true. The point of contention is the law of the excluded middle. This controversy was raised by intuitionists.

Brouwer L. E. J. (1908, 1923), the inventor of intuitionism, denies the absolute validity of the law of the excluded middle. He says that it is applicable for finite sets, but there is no guarantee that the law is applicable for infinite sets.

Suppose x has infinite range. Then we have no possibility to test whether the predicate P(x) or the predicate not P(x) exists. The law says that there can be only either P(x) or not P(x), but neither P(x) nor not P(x) can be found with certainty in some finite steps in the infinite range of x. For the same reason the validity of *reductio ad adsurdum* is doubtful for infinite sets, for this can only establish the double negation of a predicate but does not give a valid existential assertion of P(x). These ideas have formed the basis of intuitionistic mathematics, which sticks to the constructive line, i.e. instead of accepting or conceiving sets of objects of arbitrary nature it is trying to provide some principles of construction for mathematical objects.

In the intuitionist's view the law of the excluded middle is no more than a formula in the predicate calculus. The infinite series of the natural numbers may serve as an interpretation, contents of the variables of this formula. Hence we simply establish that the range of the formula should be limited with finite sets, just because we are not sure of members of the infinite series to satisfy the formula – we do not know what kind of members there could be – a member must be "constructed".

But the law of the excluded middle may be regarded as a part of a very thorough definition of distinctness of a term. When we say that a term is distinct, we imply that to be sure that it is there must be nothing but the term and what it is not, in particular.

On the other hand, the natural numbers are generated by distinctness. To call the natural numbers is to test terms as distinct. And this concerns also any other numbers – all kinds of them are merely terms, besides they are conceived with the help of the notion of the natural numbers.

Terms of natural language are anything but not infinite, in the sense that infinity in natural language is not – and by no means could be – something which is actually realized, though it can be successfully expressed. It is sufficient to describe a procedure (or what may be called so), which leads to infinity. In natural language "infinity" is always a description of a procedure, if any. In particular, the description of procedure leading to infinity is the natural numbers or any other numbers based on the conception of the natural numbers. Infinity is an abstraction for a language speaker and will never be anything but this – not only will it never be realized for him (or for them), but it is also not realized in language.

It seems highly dubious that infinity may be thought to exist on sets (hypothetical) whose members are not distinct. For if terms are not distinct, we cannot say, for a given procedure, whether they are infinite or not. Thus, suppose we have some procedure giving A, B, C, D,.... then we are confronted with the term B, indistinguishable from B of the series: A, B, C, D, B.... If we cannot say which B is this – we cannot say whether this is the successor of A or this is the successor of D – we cannot say whether the infinite series is broken or not. To determine infinite procedure having indistinct terms is very problematic or not possible at all. All descriptions of the procedures leading to infinity, which have been given here – that of the natural numbers and that of sets, are based on the notion of distinct term.

Both the law of the excluded middle and the natural numbers (or any other procedure to infinity) is based on the notion of the distinct terms. Evidently, to reject the law or the numbers would be contradictory. We cannot be sure that terms are distinct without the possibility to test each term to each – the order which can generate numbers; as well, it is hard to call a term distinct having something middle or over itself and what it is distinct from – we could not determine distinctness in this case. Deduction of the law of the excluded middle and the notion of natural numbers from that of the distinct terms has the character of development of the idea of distinctness. In our view to reject the law of the excluded middle means to revise the notion of distinctness itself, hence to alter the definitions of the procedure leading to *an* infinity based on that notion. It seems that somebody who wishes to reject the law should be ready to delineate these alterations in the definitions. Being restrained to assert the validity of the excluded middle most probably should involve being ready for changes in the definitions of procedures which provide infinity, and it seems highly difficult to conceive what kind of changes it might actually be. Thus, if we know that there may be something which is not three and at the same time which is not what is not three, then what can we say about three? In our view, if we do not reject such questions as senseless, we can only say that three and, on the other hand, all that is not three under this condition have become vague, indistinct. Hardly any other reasonable assertions may follow.

If members of the series in a procedure are indistinct, we cannot say that the procedure can provide infinity. But having no infinity, we could not have any ground to reject the law (we could check *in possibility* all x for which whether $P(x)$ or not $P(x)$). On the other hand, it is if we reject the law of the excluded middle, we make the meanings of the terms indistinct.

This shows that ideas on which intuitionism is based are merely mathematical abstractions. We can construct mathematics where the formula "whether $P(x)$ or not $P(x)$" is not satisfied for infinite sets, but we cannot *actually* lose the law of the excluded middle in the infinity. These ideas have no philosophical content. They do not show the limits of the logical law because they really do not point at the law at all.

Logical laws are constructed in the way required by the terms of language. Terms are distinct and the laws of logic are the explanation of what means to be distinct. The laws are valid for all kinds of things, no matter real or imaginary, for this limit is pointed out by language – they must be in all we say, and they are such as the way we must say it allows.

Inferences

As it was said, in the language of distinct terms iteration may be marked to make another term look different, i. e. for A A language is able to provide signs turning the terms of the expression distinct, e. g. A A*, or A AB, etc. But the requirement of distinctness does not involve restrictions on means which allow similar terms to be distinguished from each other. Terms of the series A, A, A. ....may be simply considered as having been put at different moments, in different places of the sheet of paper, etc.; they may be marked, as we have just done (with * or B); and when a distinct term happens to be repeated, it may be simply substituted by another distinct term which is single, i. e. A, A may be substituted for B (as well, in A, A one of "A"s may be substituted and the other remains).

When we add an index to a term, this is a grammatical connection. A grammatical connection should also exist between the substituted and what is substituting. And it seems that it hardly can be only that itself that "AA must be substituted by B". Indexing is just adding in order to discern one term from another – and the latter is merely the single form of the grammatical connection (in the sense we are using this notion). Adding indexes of any arbitrary lengths is still nothing but adding. By substitution it may happen that AA is substituted by B. Or it may happen that A in . . D, A, C.... and A in ....L, A, N.... connected one to the other in their terms are substituted by something different than A and different than D, C, L, N.... But can it be so that A in .... D, A, C.... and A in . . L, A, N.... when connected are substituted exactly for D, C, L, N (in any succession)? We should admit this possibility if we put no restrictions on the way terms show their distinctness.

A term may encounter (in a grammatical connection) a composed term which contains the term; then, in the composed term, all other terms but that term are that which substitute the iteration. That is, there is A, L, N.... and there is A, then we yield L, N.... as A A. (From now on, let us designate other terms but that which is iterated in the composed term as one term, i. e. let us designate L, N....as, say, B. That is, B substitutes AA).

Two composed terms may contain the same term: A, B and A, C. In their grammatical connection we yield that B, C substitutes the iteration AA.

We have connected a composed term and a single term, a composed term and another composed term, and the same single terms were replaced by the rest. That is, iteration has been "destroyed", "annihilated" by the terms it has been connected with.

Now we have the last alternative: a single term to be connected to the same single term, i.e. A and A. Can we say that AA are annihilated, as in the case of composed terms? It seems we cannot. We cannot say that iterations in language are annihilated simply because we have to say that they "are annihilated". Rather we can (and must) say that terms, if iterated, cannot disappear in literal sense of the word, but they can be replaced by terms different to them – these replacing terms may be already mentioned, as in the case of composed terms, or they may not yet be mentioned. Language has no holes, nor cavities, nor lacunas.

Suppose we have A and B grammatically connected in some way. Then we connect A to them. But this is iteration of A, i.e. AA and B. We may say that B substitutes the iterated A, i.e. AA. In other words, we are in the right to assert that if we have A and B, and A, there must be some grammatical connections among all the three terms where B may be regarded as the term which substitutes the term AA. Thus we have only B.

But such a grammatical connection is well acquainted. It is if A then B, and A; then B. This is modus ponens.

Suppose we have A and B grammatically connected in some way. And we have A and C in some way grammatically connected. And suppose both expressions have a connection to each other. Then we are in the right to say that this connection may provide that the terms B, C substitute the iteration containing in the connection of both expressions, AA. Thus we yield B, C.

The connection that makes B, C be given from A, B and A, C may be the following: A is B and A is C, then B is C. And this is recognizable as a syllogism. The connection A, B, and A, C, where AA may be replaced by BC is a schema of all modi and figures of syllogism. Syllogisms are various connections of the terms A, B, A, C, which the Grammar allows representing as BC, with the terms "all", "some", "one", "not".

We suppose that if AA is given, then there is some B to substitute AA. But we also suppose that if some B is given, then there is some AA. Thus, if there is A and B, but there is no B, then there is no A, too. If there is "if A then B" but there is no B, then there is no A – this is modus tollens.

The term AA (these may be iterating events) should be anything but A(this may be a hypothesis on the appearing of those events) – "not A" is something unmentioned in AA. But the term AAB (or the term AABC) should be B (or should be BC) – it should be something already mentioned, something already known. Inferences of this kind cannot contain something new in conclusion; for, unlike in the case of AA (as iterating events), we are dealing with deductive inferences.

Summary

What can we never do in language? The response is able to summarize all that has been written above. We shall never utter what we have uttered. This answer is unlikely to cause any controversy.

If we never utter what we have uttered, then any uttered term A will never be any term A we are now uttering and this one will never be that A we are uttering again, etc. The sequence A A A.... is the sequence of different, not the same, terms. The notion of sameness of terms is not absolute; it is relative, e. g. the terms A, A, A. . . are the same as the signs of the same shape or sounds of the same tone etc., the terms A and B are the same in the sense that they both are letters. But terms are different in an absolute sense.

This difference does not depend on the subject's will. The subject may ignore how to distinguish terms or defy recognizing that they are necessarily distinct, but terms which he puts with intention to be indistinguishable will mean different things, even if he is trying to ascribe to them the same meaning. Iteration alters the meaning of the term. Since terms are different, to connect one term to another means to alter the term, no matter whether the term which we connect is the same as the other or different from it. Thus, this difference of terms implies what terms are, what they themselves imply and what it means to connect them. That is why we call this difference in question *the Grammar*.

The subject, putting down or uttering terms A, A, A ...., actually puts down different terms. Asserting that A = A, we imply only that we could choose another way of designation than A, A, A .... – namely we might have chosen A, B, C.... To connect one term to another means to change the meaning and, strictly speaking, change the term – no matter whether "the same" or a different term is grammatically connected. The term AB is different to A and the term AA is different to A. In order to choose a designation adequate to what the concept of Grammar says we, having been confronted with AA, may replace AA for AB (that is, replace the other A for B), and we equally may replace AA for B or anything different from A. We also can establish the rule saying that AA generates a term different from A. In this case the required distinctness is held: if AA generates B, we may replace AA for B or AA for AB, or we may have all terms possibly arisen from the rule: A, AB, B, keeping within the requirement.

It has long been known that in order to prove that (A, B) =(C, D) if A=C and B=D, we must present (A, B) as A, A, B (respectively with (C, D) and the same must be said about, e.g. (A, B, F)). Thus we infer that if A A (generates) B, then A B (strictly in this order); and so for "if AABAABF then ABF", etc.

On the other hand, to satisfy the requirement of distinctness we take a term, then another and test whether it is distinct from the first, then another and test whether it is distinct from the first and from the second, etc. It is the testing of distinctness from each other that makes the succession – one is the successor of the other. This testing is similar by nature to counting. In this testing any terms participate in definite order. The natural numbers are the special names for testing of this kind. Both the succession made out of AABAABF and the latter succession is nothing but A, B, F....

Obviously, the rule "AA generates B" generates sets with their subsets when the terms it generates by iteration are as well iterated again and again:

A A (B) B A A(B) B   C....

The subject may deem to utter a sequence of the same terms, yielding *actually* different. And on another level, the subject may make no explicit mention that an iterated term must not be that term – that AA is not A, as it is the case in the axioms of a formal system or in its rules of inference. Nevertheless the system may have terms based on iterations as expressible in the system without, though, being able to determine their truth or falsehood by its own means. This is the case with undecidable propositions (in particular with the Continuum Hypothesis) in formal arithmetic (or in set theory).

If the subject neglects that in language the term AA is anything but A, he arrives at logical or semantical (both have turned out to be of the same nature) paradoxes.

The three laws of thought are explainable by the notion of distinctness of terms. And laws of inferences and syllogisms of deductive logic are nothing but substitutions of AA by terms already mentioned in the contexts where AA appears. In inductive logic the conclusions that substitute AA may not be contained in such contexts but, obviously, the conclusions are not what the iterations are.

To think logically means to practice the Grammar – the Grammar is first, then logic.

Extending Terms

Until now we have been regarding only one kind of terms, the ones of which we know that they are distinct from each other. It was our assumption that language consisted of them. Language is what has means to distinguish its terms. But, obviously, this assumption itself is based on the distinguishing of the two kinds of terms, the ones which can be distinguished one from another and the ones that cannot be distinguished in such a way. Thus, since we are distinguishing terms, we must add to all the terms we are distinguishing from each other the terms which cannot be distinguished one from another of their own kind (from the hypothetical terms indistinguishable for us), but which for that very reason must be distinguished from the terms of the opposite kind, i.e. those which can be distinguished one from another. Adding in this *term* (for us this term is the one, for it cannot be discernable from the ones of its own kind) seems quite reasonable.

A term which does not differ from another term (or could not be discerned from another) differs from the terms which differ one from another simply for the reason that it is a term of the other kind. So it should be introduced into the set of terms which are different one from another. But surely we cannot introduce other terms of that kind as discernable ones, as those to which we can refer as *distinct* in the same sense as all other distinct terms of language. Strictly speaking in the set of terms which are different one from another there can be only one term belonging to the set of terms of which we could not say that they are distinct from each other, for this is the one we simply can distinguish as "Indistinguishable among its own kind".

The set of terms which we can discern as different from one another is the following: A, B, C, DF, ERT, L, HG, F, etc....And the set of terms which we cannot distinguish one from another may be only the following: X, X, X, X, X, X.... And what we deem to be in the right to do is to add A, B, C, DF, ERT, L, HG, F, etc. to X. We yield the following: A, B, C, DF, ERT, L, HG, F, X, etc. But we cannot yield literally A, B, C, DF, ERT, L, HG, F, etc., X, X, X, X .... For this would contradict the requirement of the Grammar – all that we have added to the distinct terms is "the term that cannot be distinguished among the terms of its kind".

The term X must have properties, which differ from the properties of the terms of the opposite set. If we encounter A and A we are sure that language has means to distinguish A and A. In order to indicate that A, connected to A must have different meaning than A, we may replace A A by some other term than A, say, by B. Or we may mark another A to indicate its difference from A, e. g., like that: A (B)A. Or, as it is done by counting, we may mark each similar object: (C)A (B)A.

But the fact that X is taken from the set where terms cannot be distinguished makes its *connections* with the distinguishable terms different from those which have been described. Thus, if we encounter X and X, we cannot say that some A can replace them, for meanings of X and X X are indistinguishable. As well, we cannot mark another X by A: (A)X, for the principle that "to distinguish means to make marks" is not applicable here. In both cases if X X are given and A is connected, we can have only A X. And that is all we can distinguish. Neither marking nor rules like "A A generates B" are applicable. It does not follow from X X that it must be designated in some other way than X. And we are not able to use A to make X and X different. A, X, X is neither A, (A)X, X; nor simply (A)X, X. But A, X, X can only be A, X. As well, no counting can make different what is not able to be distinguished. Encountering X X we cannot discern that it is X and X but not X. Marking X X by A and B, i. e. (A)X (B)X, we nevertheless yield A B X.

       Now it is clear that we have:
       a) A X X is equal to A X, and
       b) AX BX is equal to A B X.
       Then, from our definition of X we infer:
       c) A is included in AX.

But this means that if we had defined empty set for our set of the distinct terms (a term that would designate what "empty set" or the zero-sign is to designate), then we could assert that the set of the distinct terms was closed.

We have stated that language has no "empty spaces", i.e. nothing in language is always "nothing", but it does not mean that we deny the role in language of the term which we usually designate as "empty set" or "0".

We assume that if we connect a term to a term which is different to it, we yield a term which differs from both the former and the latter: A and B is AB, and A is no B and each of them is no AB. We also assume that A and A are by no means A. But suppose the term 0. Let us define that 0 does not alter the terms it is connected to (unlike our distinct terms): A and 0 is A, and 0 and 0 is always 0. If the terms A B C.... are distinct, then the terms A B C.... 0 are also distinct; in particular, the term 0 is distinct from the terms A B C.... for, unlike them, it does not alter terms in connections. The definition of 0 does not contradict to the assumption of distinctness. It is defined so that it does not clash the distinctness of A B C .... and at the same time it is distinct from each of them, as each of them is to be.

Thus we add the empty set – i.e. the term whose way to connect to other terms differs from the way other terms do connect one to another – to our set of the distinct terms. Obviously, in order to assert that the union of the set of the distinct terms and of the empty set is closed, it makes sense to determine the empty set as having its own closure, i. e. as being closed to itself:

d) 0 is equal to OX.

a), b), c) and d) allow us to say that the set of terms 0 A B C.... X is closed. They also allow us to say that the terms 0 A B C....X constitute a topological space.

We identify points of a topological space as distinct. Points are indivisible objects, they have no parts. To divide means to distinguish various parts. A point is that which ends any distinguishing – one cannot distinguish further than a point allows. Thus, if we are able to distinguish anything, we are able to distinguish points and their collections. We assume that terms are that which designates points and their collections.

Terms as "Points"

Suppose the subject realizes that the terms he is uttering: A, A, A.... are to be regarded as different despite looking similar. Suppose even that he recognizes it having been acquainted with the concept of the Grammar. Our question is: How does the subject know that terms are different? Does he simply admit that they must be distinct by nature disregarding any similarity as not relevant or not essential, or the realization of distinctness should consist in having some devices which allow marking distinct signs or substituting similar-looking signs or converting them into those appearing as distinct? But it seems that there cannot be anything distinct without possibility to distinguish. If we assume that terms are distinct, we must imply that we have means to express the difference of each of them from the others. Thus, if terms A, A, A....are found out, which are not distinguished one from another, we beforehand have means that help them to become distinguishable.

If the subject realizes that terms A, A, A.... are distinct, it means that he has in mind their distinctions – they might be different places on the sheet of paper they are written, different moments of time they are put, etc. If the distinctions are unknown to the subject – say, no real place or time or any data might have been registered, then the subject's language provides them with distinctions of any form. For language's Grammar consists in connecting terms which cannot mean what the ones they are connected to must mean. So to say, language is what generates distinctions of different sorts.

Saying that terms are distinct we are saying that we can provide distinctions. But we are not saying that terms may be distinct without having distinctions.

Counting is universal distinctions. Assigning numbers of the count, we are making counted things – which are designated by one and the same term – be distinct. As it has been already asserted, counting or the natural numbers are just terms of language themselves once tested or established as distinct each from the others, which makes the succession and are usually represented as special signs. Testing or establishing distinctness of each term from the others implies that we can only establish a definite quantity of such terms. If we encounter or generate by some made out procedure similar terms, we have at our disposal strictly as many marks or distinctions for those similar terms as we can establish by this testing.

Suppose we have tested that the terms A B C D E F are distinct. And the result of a procedure is K K K K K K..... We can distinguish similar terms of the procedure insofar as we have tested terms which are to serve as distinctions or marks. K K K K K K.... may be distinguished as (A)K (B)K (C)K (D)K (E)K (F)K.... If we had only A B C as tested, we could not distinguish K K K K K K ....properly, we could yield only (A)K (B)K (C)K K K K..... ; K K K would not be discernible (unlike (A)K (B)K (C)K). But it cannot be so. The number of instances cannot exceed the number of distinctions. A procedure may be said to be infinite, but the instances we actually can present – our language is not infinite – cannot outnumber the number of distinctions we are assigning to them, in particular the number of instances we can present is not more than the natural numbers we can present as their numerals (if the numerals are to be only the natural numbers).

No matter how we are advanced in actual or virtual counting, we always arrive at some definite number n. And it is just having this n natural numbers that we can distinguish signs of real numbers up to n-th sign.

Thus, if we have n numbers and have no other signs of distinctions, we can discern up to n-th "9" in the real number 0,99999....

Suppose we have tested the terms A B C D . . . up to the term N. Then by way of various procedures we construct expressions out of those terms: ABC, CD, AAC, CCCCC, etc.... We can distinguish terms which are iterating in those expressions up to the term (in the tested terms) N. In the expression CCCCCCCC....we distinguish "C"s in the following way: (A)C, (B)C, (C)C....(N)C. We cannot distinguish more than N terms which are iterating in expressions.

And if we have established that the terms A B C D.... are distinct one to the others up to the term M, then we can discern in the iterations (in any of them occur) the terms up to M, not more: (A)C, (B)C, (C)C....(M)C. Establishing A B C D.... M distinctions we have guaranteed that the requirement of the Grammar will be satisfied. If we have established A B C.... M distinctions, it would be nonsensical to speak of other iterations than those to be "covered" by A B C.... M. For in language there must be means to distinguish a term from a term even if they look similar. The tested terms ABC.... M (the natural numbers) are called universal distinctions, for they are not casual, they guarantee for iterating terms to be provided with distinction signs to show that the requirement of the Grammar is satisfied. If there are distinctions, then the terms are distinct. The guarantee to have distinctions is to establish terms whose distinctness one from another is tested successively one by one, i. e. to make the distinctness of a term itself means to serve as a distinction sign (to "create" the natural numbers). This way we can have N guaranteed distinctions (those which cannot *be or not be*, but can only *be*). And having N distinctions (a definite number of them) we can generate various expressions applying various procedures. Otherwise, the distinctness of generated expressions (or terms) cannot be guaranteed.

Can we now conclude from the above speculations that terms of language constitute Euclidean space?

The points of Euclidean space are various real-valued functions defined on the set of the first n natural numbers.

The grammatical connections of terms may be restricted to the ones to constitute Euclidean space with n dimensions. This is to be a part of the points (or corresponding terms) in the space with arbitrary many dimensions.

In language we are composing various terms out of other terms: ABC, AABG, GL, HHH, etc.... The composed terms may be generated in accordance with a procedure which says that composing must be infinite: AAAAA...., or it may say that a composed term must be finite. The procedures which say about the compositions may be various; it may be the rule of subject and predicate or a mathematical rule on the calculus of infinitesimals. In order to satisfy the requirement of the Grammar we must have some terms whose distinctness from each other is tested: A B C D... – it is possible to test this up to the term N – and which, connected to the terms in the compositions which otherwise are indiscernible, may serve as guaranteed distinctions, i.e. distinction signs which may be applied to all sorts of terms, and which are available up to N. (Obviouly, the concept of the Grammar cannot presuppose something that would prevent to use these tested terms in any composed terms, for they are distinct). We may admit that the tested terms A B C D . . . correspond to the natural numbers (up to n, if the terms are established up to N), and the composed terms correspond to the real-valued functions. But the real-valued functions is a kind of such composed terms and their values can replace the terms; as well, A B C D....N is another designations for the natural numbers up to n.

If we had admitted on some metaphysical reasons that terms might have been distinct without that the subject could always name their distinctions, we could not have asserted that terms of language could correspond to the points of Euclidean space. But we did admit the contrary. To construct a point in Euclidean space we are to consider its dimensions, "parameters" which are numbering to n. To construct terms out of other terms which are to be distinct we are to know – if we are considering the requirement of distinctness – to what "extent" their distinctness is spread. That is, we must be sure that guaranteed "measure" within which we discern terms is A B C.... up to N (and this "measure" is the greatest).

The Distinguishing Function

If we assume that terms of language are distinct, we can also assume that terms may be represented as points. But terms may be also represented as values of a function that makes any terms – the same, as well as different – be distinct from each other.

The domain of this function is various iterating and different terms: N, D, LK, A, ABC.... G, ABC, U, P, A .... And the values are only different terms: N, D, LK, A, ABC, C, ABC*, U P, (B)A, ... An iterating term, e.g. AA, may be turned into distinct in any mode: AA may be substituted for AB, or AA may be substituted for A and AB, or AA may be substituted for B – all the modes are considered as the same function.

We have said that the succession of the natural numbers arises from checking the difference of one term from all others. We take a term (or sign), check its difference from all other signs, and this determine the place of the sign in the succession. But evidently, this procedure is implied by the notion of the function which is making all sorts of terms distinct. If such a function is given, then it is implied that if we have A B C D and they are distinct, and we are to learn whether Z is distinct, we have to compare Z with each of A B C D (i. e. whether A=Z, B=Z, C=Z, D=Z or not); and so is for Y, if A B C D Z are distinct. This succession is giving the notion of "less or bigger" – earlier or later checking. In particular, the natural numbers are based on this procedure and all kinds of numbers which are based on the natural numbers, e. g. the real numbers, are determined by it.

Every term has its place in this succession but one. This is the term X, i.e. the term which is distinct from the terms of the succession because, unlike the latter ones, it is taken from the set whose terms cannot be distinguished one from another (it represents all that can be taken from this set, for to be "undistinguished from the others" is the single characteristic of all the terms of this set).

To be less or bigger means to have this or that place in the succession in which the comparison of terms is being done. X is always "less or bigger" than the terms of the succession because it need not be in the succession to be known as distinct. This is the nature of its distinctness.

And since the term X is "less or bigger" than other terms, we should conclude that the set of the distinct terms may be regarded as bounded by X. That is, A B C.... is bounded by X; and since the set 0 is so defined that each A B C.... contains 0 and 0 is 0 X, then the set 0 and the set A B C.... are bounded by X.

The function whose values are 0 A B C D.... is bounded. And the set of the distinct terms is a bounded set.

The function is making the terms of the domain – whether different or the same within the domain – distinct. Thus, the values of the function are terms, which are distinct from each other; i.e. the terms are only distinct as the values. For any term from among the values there are any number of the terms (from the values) which are only distinct from each other and all of them from the term. And all of those terms (the latter one and the former ones) are made out of the terms of the domain (distinct or not). Any number of the terms which are the values is necessarily corresponding to the according number of the terms of the domain.

Since we assumed that points, as well as terms of language, are distinct, we may express the said above in the following way. For each point of the domain x and for any arbitrary neighborhood of y ($y=f(x)$, where f is the function in question and y is a point of the values), there is an adequate neighborhood of x, which is entirely mapped into the given neighborhood of y, in accordance with the function f. Points of the neighborhood of x are not necessarily distinct; but the mapping is such that they are adequate (in the sense of the mapping) to any arbitrary neighborhood of y, whose points are necessarily distinct; and this is valid for all of x.

It should bring us to the conclusion that the function – the function that turns any terms into distinct one to another – is continuous.

Other Modes of Connections

Earlier we have established that generally to be distinct means to have distinctions. If terms weren't to serve as universal distinctions – i. e. the natural numbers, they would not be distinct at all. This determines the basis for Euclidean space. Whatever we construct out of terms, we construct considering definite distinctions, a definite number. To construct a point (or, e.g., a vector in the space) we should consider a given number of coordinates. We could not speak about Euclidean space, if we could comprehend "distinct" without definite distinctions.

We have introduced the term X, which differs from other terms because it is from of the opposite set, i. e. the set whose terms cannot be distinguished one from another; and the term 0, which contains X and does not alter terms to which it is connected. This addition makes the set of the distinct terms closed.

Then we have regarded the distinct terms as values of the function which turns any terms into ones which are distinct from each other. And we have seen that this function is bounded and continuous.

But if in Euclidean space we have a closed and bounded set (i. e. we have a compact) then for every continuous function there is at least one fixed point. That is, for every continuous function $y=f(x)$ there is at least one point p, for which $f(p)=p$.

In other words, we have to recognize that for the set of the distinct terms Brouwer's fixed point theorem is valid. Our continuous function is the grammatical connections of any terms. Those connections alter terms. As we have seen, the set of the distinct terms is such that we are to apply to our function Brouwer's fixed point theorem ((1912); an exposition of the theorem may be found, e. g. in Kuratowski (1972)). That is, we are to allow that for every term A, there exists at least one term P, whose grammatical connection with A gives the term P itself, (for any A, $AP=P$).

So what have we learnt when we learn that Brouwer's fixed point theorem must be applied to the distinct terms? We learn that there must be terms (fixed points) with another mode of connection.

All terms alter when connected to each other. This provides that they are distinct. A term of language becomes (or is made) different while connecting (or connected). But since terms are distinct, we could not trespass upon their distinctness if we made up a term which would differ from others because it could not be connected, or, which is the same, would be contained in all the terms, including itself. So it is with 0 – A and 0 is A, 0 and 0 is 0. And – the other option – we could make up a term which differs from all the rest because it would not alter terms, although it may be connected to them. This is so with the term of the opposite set, with X: X can mark neither other terms nor itself, nor 0 (X0 is 0 – X does not turn 0 into something different, what "marking" should do).

But Brouwer's theorem points out that there is another kind of terms (or at least one term) with another mode of connections. Such terms are the ones where all other terms are "contained": any A and P is P. That is, 0 and P is P, A and P is P, B and P is P.... X and P is P; or (0 A B C....X) and P is P.

It is important to notice that the terms 0 A B C.... X were assumed. We established that all terms were distinct and ascribed to them the according grammar. Then we introduced some special terms (0 and X). They differ from all other terms in respect of their grammatical connections and their characteristics were to be specially determined not to break the general property of distinctness. Such terms could not be any and their characteristics must be given having considered the characteristics (the mode of the grammatical connection) of all other terms; unlike the latter terms, such terms are to be named ("the empty set", "a member of the set with indistinguishable members") – since the mode of connections is not the same, their distinctness should be determined specially.

But fixed points (or a fixed point, the term P), are not assumed. They are deduced. We establish that terms of language must be distinct. Then find out what terms must be if they are distinct. We yield 0 A B C D.... X. Then considering Brouwer's fixed point theorem, we conclude that the account of elements of the set of the distinct terms is not exhausted by the terms 0 A B C D....X, the set of the distinct terms must also contain P. The existence of 0 A B C D....X necessarily implies the existence of P.

We deduced from the supposition that terms are distinct, that there are terms which "contain" all other terms, in the sense that if Z is any term, there is at least one term P, such that Z, grammatically connected to P, is P itself. In a sense, distinctness of any terms one from another implies their "disappearance" in certain definite terms.

Thus, in the Grammar, terms 0 A B C D.... X are such and are in such relations that they require the addition of the term P (at least one) – the latter is dependent of the former ones in the above said way.

The Fixed Point Theorem

The full version of Brouwer's fixed point theorem is proved for the n-dimensional ball. Simpler and less general versions are given for a circle on the plane. The version of the theorem proved for a closed interval is of even less generality but even easier.

The latter proof is based on the idea of closed intervals which are inserted one into another. If there are infinite number of such intervals each lying within the previous, then they obviously have their common point. When dividing the closed interval we do not find out the fixed point – e.g. on an end of one of the inserted intervals – after a finite number of steps of such division, then this common point is the fixed point of the continuous mapping of the closed interval into itself. This immediately follows from the continuity. Suppose the contrary. Suppose that the continuous mapping of the interval into itself has no fixed point – this common point is no fixed point, i. e. f(x) = y and y is not equal to x. The continuity implies that for any neighborhood of y there is a neighborhood of x whose points have their images in the neighborhood of y. Let us take the neighborhood of y to be so narrow that the two neighborhoods do not intersect. And let us take the inserted interval to be so narrow that it all is lying in the neighborhood of x, i.e. in the common point's neighborhood. This means that all the points of the inserted interval are moved to the side where the neighborhoods of y are lying. But this contradicts the idea of inserted intervals – to the way the closed interval was divided, for the ends of any inserted interval must move in different directions, namely to the inside. Hence the common point x is the fixed point of the mapping.

We have given a sketchy proof of the fixed point theorem as it is usually done, and we also could give the generalized proofs for figures with more dimensions than an interval has.

But we do not need to carry out a special proof using the concept of the distinct terms, in the terminology of the distinct terms immediately. For real numbers are also terms of language. Besides they can perfectly serve as terms of ordinary language in quite ordinary circumstances, say, in codes. And points of a usual topological space are identified as objects which can be potentially distinguished one from another – it is supposed that this is the reason why there cannot be something "less" than a point. All we have to do is to conceive a set of terms which cannot be distinguished and add to the set of the distinct terms a term from the former set (using its only possible characteristic of being from the set of indistinguishable terms). And this gives the basis for the assertion that if we have the set of the distinct terms, then there must be "fixed" terms: 0 A B C D....X implies P.

It seems quite legitimate to admit that terms are adequate to points. Terms are primitives of language (in the interpretation of them assumed in the concept of the Grammar) and points are primitives for a part of language and as such, as primitives of that part, they are all that they constitute, and the same with the terms of language. To compose a term one may have any number of elementary (distinct) terms up to n – a point (or vector) may have n dimensions. Whether we have points or terms, we are dealing with objects of the same nature and we are in the right to expect that restricting them within the same conditions we yield the same results.

"Fixed Points" in Language

If language may be identified with a set of points, then this must imply that to be a point of such a set means to be potentially or actually named and to be named means to be distinguished one from another. And if we identify terms with points, which term may correspond with a fixed point?

If we admit that "f" means the grammatical connection of a certain term, can this be simply a number? – Obviously not (not for the set of terms). Numbers are terms which are subjected to the general thesis that the grammatical connections alter the meaning. This mode of connection indicates that A B is no A and no B, and A A is anything but A. Generally, connections of numbers hold this way. The exception is the empty set which is contained in or – which is the same – cannot be connected to anything: for any A, A and 0 is A, and 0 and 0 is 0. Numbers themselves are the product of the juxtaposition of terms with the mentioned mode of connection one to another in order to yield the series of different signs – the act taken as a whole makes the single series which could replace all terms.

A term which is able to designate a fixed point should be searched among ordinary terms, notions which we, most probably, use in our everyday life. At first we should just exclude all the terms with modes of connection that differ from the one of the fixed points. We must exclude our closure X, it is to be connected to any term; we must exclude the empty set, it is not to be connected to any term, i.e. A and 0 makes A; and we must exclude all other terms, the terms which alter by connections. Among ordinary terms of language we must search a term P, such as for any A, P and A is P. This must be a term which remains itself whatever can be grammatically connected to it. In a sense, this term "contains" all other terms. Suppose anything, i.e. any word, expression, sentence, either meaningful or nonsensical; in a sense, if we considered beside that our term, we could not have to consider what we had considered first.

Beside that term, anything is becoming to be that term itself.

It must be clear that a term, which having been grammatically connected to any other terms remains itself, can only denote terms in their grammatical connections. And terms in their grammatical connections are language itself.

Thus, if for any A we have a P, which having been connected to A, gives P itself, then P is language itself. A fixed point or a term which is adequate to a fixed point is "language". This is the result brought by the idea of the fixed point.

Wittgenstein's Language

But what kind of language could it be, whose idea might be represented by the concept of a fixed point? Or what do we know about language, if we know that it is essentially *a fixed point*?

As we have just said, this language represents nothing but terms in their connections. Whatever terms we add we yield language as terms added one to another through grammatical connections.

Suppose we support the idea that there exists something extra-linguistic, objects are not adequate to words, or no representation can fit the external world in principle. That is, we may say, for instance, that the external world is too complex or too subtle to be described by language, that language is too weak and impotent to picture phenomena perfectly. Thus, for instance, we may say that in language a heap and two beans, three beans, four beans etc. are not strictly distinguishable, for these all are a heap; or we may say that works of art are able to convey something to what language cannot even approach, or that there are phenomena which can have no names and we have to put up with ambiguities; and so forth. We can make similar statements on the drawbacks of such means of communication as language, no matter whether they are controversial or undiscussible, false or true. Making those statements, despite the fact that they refer to something extra-linguistic, we are to recognize that the statements of the kind are made and can only be made in language.

In other words, what we are doing is the following. We juxtapose a term denoting language and terms denoting failure of language, and we yield the resultant term denoting language. That is, terms, being grammatically connected to the term "language" (or to any of its synonyms or expressions with the same meaning), necessarily give language itself.

But what we are regarding is a particular case of "for any A, A and P is P". If we recognize that limits set by language cannot be surmounted, i.e., if we say that any assertions on a failure of language necessarily result in language itself; then we are articulating a particular case of the assertion "A and P is P", the assertion on a fixed point.

Suppose we know the flaws of language and set a task to correct it. Suppose it is discovered that it is achievable to make language stricter, exact and perspicuous, devoid of ambiguities. Natural language would be reinforced by devices making it more powerful and clear (for instance, such as different formalizations). In a sense, we may say that we possess means to explain natural language; for, in fact, we give explanations of statements of natural language. Generally, a collection of statements which treat language is meta-language.

But again, it should be recognized that actually any explanations of natural language or even construction of a meta-language for natural language can be nothing but an extension of it, i.e. can be nothing but natural language itself.

That is, in general, language, connected to a certain collection of its explanations (or being juxtaposed to its meta-language), is necessarily language itself – a particular case of "for any A, A and P is P".

Now it should be clear that the language that falls under the principle "for any A, A and P is P" (i.e. under the concept of "fixed point" in the concept of the language of the distinct terms) is the one which represents a limit which we cannot surmount, an entity that can be neither destroyed nor completed, which cannot be even explained. But it cannot be explained because it explains itself, giving any explanations of language we have to use language itself. And of course it cannot be replaced (for what could replace it? – to ascribe other meanings to words; that is, to use words in another way, changing the meaning and using words in another way does not mean to change language for something other than language itself).

It is easy to see that we are giving characteristics of Wittgenstein's language – this concept is in accordance with the concept of language given by Wittgenstein (especially in 1955, 1984, and 1989).

Roughly speaking, according to Wittgenstein, speaking about language necessarily gives language. As well, whatever we connect to "language" in the language of the distinct terms we necessarily yield "language". But this is the case when the same thought represents itself as the single result of two different approaches.

We need not adduce many of exegetical arguments in support of the assertion that Wittgenstein postulates this conception of language. For him language is an entity. It can be neither corrected nor explained without that language itself being used. The very questions on language cannot be put without language itself. Neither can we suppose to find out its basis or certain premises or principles of it without this basis representing language itself. This entity may be conceivable only as a kind of postulate, as something that cannot be deduced (it is why it is conceived as an entity).

Meanwhile in the language of distinct terms the assertion that "language" connected to any term is necessary "language", is no postulate. In this language this assertion is dependent on other assertions. In the upshot, this is a consequence of the assumption that terms of language are distinct. The distinct terms implies that the term "language", grammatically connected to any other terms, gives "language".

The language "0 A B C D....X" implies the language "0 A B C D....X P", where P is such that for any A, A and P is P. And since "for any A, A and P is P" is the expression to which the concept of Wittgenstein's language – the language, any predicating of which necessarily gives the language itself – may be reduced, then we may assert that Wittgenstein's language is secondary toward language of the distinct terms, i.e. it is deduced from it.

The language of the distinct terms implies Wittgenstein's language, as well as – and by the same reason, the language "0 A B C D.... X" implies the language "0 A B C D.... X P".

The "language" that cannot be explained because it explains itself is no postulate. *The language that explains itself* is a product of deduction.

"The Philosophical I"

Thus, "0 A B C D.....X P" follows from "0 A B C D....X". The existence of a term which may be connected to any other term and remains itself – so to say, a term which can "absorb" all other terms – follows from the assumption that terms are distinct. But the implication must say somewhat more than the declaration of the existence of a single term of the kind. There may exist other terms with the same mode of grammatical connections as P, i.e. for any A, A and P is P. For the theorem says that for any continuous function in a closed and bounded set there exists *at least* one fixed point.

Can there be other fixed points in this particular case, i.e. can there be other terms except for "language" to be identified with fixed points?

Wittgenstein (1955 p.153) prompts the answer. The famous extract runs:

> The I occurs in philosophy through the fact that "the world is my world". The philosophical I is not the man, not the human body or the human soul of which psychology treats, but the metaphysical subject, the limit – not a part of the world.

This "philosophical I" is the I of solipsism, the "self". He says further:

> In fact what solipsism means is quite correct, only it cannot be said, but shows itself. That the world is my world shows itself in the fact that the limits of the language (the language that I understand) mean the limits of my world.

Thus he asserts the difference and the similarity between solipsism and his concept of language.

The true philosophical solipsism says that whatever we perceive or conceive has to be within our I, within the self. Nothing is conceivable without the I. It seems that anybody can be convinced in it at any moment. It is what anyone can "show" to himself. Someone may object to that saying that there are things existing independently of anyone's I, things which are subjected to laws and which are out of the subject's influence or knowledge, laws which are objective. But all this is off the point. For the very objections I hear or conceive are just within my I.

"The world is my world" of solipsism means that the term "I" may be grammatically connected to any other term. "The world is my world" implies that to talk about I means to talk about the world, for we cannot say that there exists something without the I. On the other hand, hardly anyone can "show" himself his I without the world – no "limit" is conceivable without what it limits.

Anything conceived or perceived (imaginary or real) is "labeled" by the I. It may be said that the I implies whatever – no part but a limit of the world, something that "confines" all the existing (existing in any form, imaginary or not: in any mode or modality, possible or necessary, etc.). Regarding that anything cannot exist without the I, it may be said that anything may be "replaced" by the I . In the sense that "the world is my world"; the I is what implies (or confines) the entire world. In this sense "the world is my world" is a particular case of "for any A, A and P is P".

Thus, it seems, we have two terms identified with a fixed point – one is "language", another is the I. From the language (0 A B C D....X) we yield the language with at least two fixed points: (0 A B C D.....X P* P**), where P* is language and P** is the I.

The Paradox of Language

An attentive reader should have noticed a serious flaw in our speculations.

We have discussed the concept of language as identified with a "fixed point". We have found out that this concept is Wittgensteinean. And this means that language is an entity that can be neither corrected nor completed nor replaced nor explained by any other entity except itself. It cannot be derived from anything else; it is what is just given. This is what should be meant when the term "language" is used.

But the point is that the term "language", with this very meaning of it, was deduced from what was represented as the distinct terms!

We have assumed that language consists of the distinct terms. Then, led by natural considerations, we have added to those terms the single term 0 and the single term X, which, though, having their own type of the grammatical connections, do not contradict the assumption of distinctness. And this urges us to conclude, doing further natural assumptions, such as identification of terms and points of topological space, that there must be another type of terms, the terms "P". And this term P (to be more exact P*) is language as the entity described by Wittgenstein, the one that cannot be explained.

We have explained what is not to be explainable (for it explains itself, so to say, it has already been (or is) explained by itself); we have derived what is not to be derivable!

We have stated that if (0 A B C D....X) then P. But P is such that P is anything connected to P. Thus, 0 A B C D....X P must be P. We deduced what by its very nature must not be deduced; for hardly can be found anything more general than something implying to be itself, once having been added to anything. Suppose that Y is more general, but P is such that P and Y is P – P is no "part" of the world.

All this means that our implication "if (0 A B C D....X) then (0 A B C D....X P)" is nonsensical. The language 0 A B C D....X P derives its own underivability. It explains its own unexplainability; or, which is the same, asserting self-sufficiency of the fact that it explains itself, this language contradicts itself giving explanation of this, therefore breaking the self-sufficiency.

The Dilemma of Language

How could we manage to obtain such disconcerting result? Can this be a product of some mistake in speculations, i.e. having correct premisses we have made erroneous inferences? But it is difficult to make many mistakes in an inference containing no complex technicalities. Can our premiss be wrong? In other words, can the concept of the Grammar[1] be invalid?

The latter can be admitted, but there are many logical phenomena which are fit for the Grammar of language, i.e. it explains a lot. It is not easy to reject a concept in whose terms we may speak about the number and about the laws of logic, having it as the basis of them; a concept that, unlike formal theories, does consider iterations, on which undecidable propositions are based.

Furthermore, language, in accordance with the Grammar, cannot generate paradoxes.

But it is now clear that having fled from the paradoxes arising in language we have arrived at another paradox. This paradox seems to be more serious, it concerns language itself. In other words, the concept of the Grammar consequently allows us to assert that language itself is paradoxical. To accept that terms of language are distinct means resultantly to recognize that language contains a contradiction in itself, that language by its very nature is what derives the underivable.

If we do not accept that terms of language are necessarily distinct (or if we do not accept the Grammar of language), then we may not recognize that iteration of a term, generally speaking, must necessarily constitute a term which is different from those the iteration consists of (or we may not recognize that AA is not necessary not A). In particular, we may not recognize that "set of sets" is no set, or "barber for the barber" is not a barber, or "specification of the specification" is not a specification, etc.; to contrary, we may consider a set of sets to be a set and a barber for the barber to be a barber. This way we inevitably come to the conclusion that language whose terms are not distinct – iteration has the same meaning as its single member – contains insoluble contradictions, paradoxes. And avoiding paradoxes in formal theories, we yield propositions in them, of which a theory cannot say whether they are true or false, while the construction of those propositions is based on iterations.

If we do accept that terms of language are necessarily distinct – if we do accept that AA is necessary not A, we soon find out that there exist terms which, as well as others, are distinct from others, though they are distinct for the reason that they do not connect to terms as others do (as AA is not A) – those terms are 0 and X. Then it is not so hard to notice that we are dealing with the premises which conclude, through the theorem, the existence of the term P, which immediately leads to the recognition that we derive the underivable and explain the unexplainable.

It seems that all the steps leading from the acceptance of the assumption that terms of language are distinct to the assertion of deriving the underivable are justified, and we are now confronted with a choice. We are to choose between the language containing contradictions and the language whose very concept is contradictory.

The choice to be made is arbitrary; it is not influenced by anything but the subject's will or the subject's taste. Our steps from the assumption of distinctness to the assertion that language itself is contradictory were compelling. The conclusion we have made is based on logically plausible reasons. But now it turns out that the choice between the rejection of distinctness on one hand and the recognition that the concept of language itself is contradictory is a matter of taste.

A reason why we could prefer to reject distinctness is that in the opposite case we would feel that we arrived at a total absurdity. Without distinctness we have the language able to generate certain contradictions. While accepting distinctness, we have to state that what we are doing – stating anything while using language – is absurd only because what we are doing is using language; and to state the contrary or something different or anything is absurdity nevertheless. Thus we could choose language without the assumption of distinctness of its terms, language with paradoxes, as smaller evil. But this choice is not in agreement with the compulsion of logical inferences, rather this is a question of the subject's preference.

Notes

1. What we are calling here "the Grammar" may be characterized as non-linearity of language. This terminology arises from the division of all languages into linear and non-linear. We may call natural language non-linear because it does not admit repetitions of a symbol. H.B. Curry in his *Foundations of Mathematical Logic* (1963. p.30) defines a linear language: "Generally the expressions are

arbitrary linear series of letters in which repetitions may occur; in that case the language will be called a linear language. Thus in the linear language whose alphabet consists of the three letters: a, b, c, the following are examples of expressions: a, abca, bcccaa, abcbabcccaa".

Another Mode of Connection

Can we try to find a way out of this impasse? Is there any solution of the paradox of language? I.e. the solution of the assertion that language is what derives the underivable, of the assertion that the language 0 A B C D....X implies the language O A B C D....X P?

The first that occurs is that we could try to treat the paradox of language as we do with other paradoxes. But this is obviously erroneous.

For the terms with whose help the paradoxes are constructed have another mode (or fashion) of the grammatical connection than the term "language" has. The terms A B C D.... are connected one to another in another way than the term P is made. If A is connected to A or B is connected to B, etc., we yield, correspondingly, anything but A and anything but B etc.... That is, a barber for the barber is anything but not a barber and a characteristic of the characteristic is anything but not a characteristic, etc. But we cannot say the same about P. It seems that P and A is P even if A is P. We cannot say that natural language can be described by anything which is not itself or is not derived from natural language itself – natural language connected to anything is natural language, or it consists of itself and anything else. The paradox of language is a paradox of another nature than the ones we know how to construct (or, which is the same, how to solve). Paradoxes arise from mistaking the iteration with a single term. The paradox of language arises from the fact that in language it is possible to deduce a term which by its very nature (mode of connection) cannot be deduced.

The language of the distinct terms does not give us means to solve the paradox of language. It gives means to solve, and hence to construct, other paradoxes; but it cannot give the solution of the paradox that concerns itself – the language of the distinct terms is the construction that *itself* represents this paradox.

The Metaphysical Solution

But if there are no means and no idea of the solution, could there be some justification to leave it without any solution?

We have concluded that language is contradictory; the concept of language is what is derivable and at the same time not, i.e. it is and it is not at the same time and in the same sense. That is, language breaks the law of non-contradiction. But the logical law of non-contradiction is exposed above as a consequence of the concept of the Grammar. We can mean things insofar as we use terms. If terms can be only distinct, they can designate only distinct things, if any. That a term is distinct implies that it can be either the term itself or any of those from what it is distinct; and it can designate only what is either itself or not itself – we cannot express something which can be both itself and not itself with a distinct term.

Should something that gives basis to the law of non-contradiction itself be itself necessarily non-contradictory? A justification should be justified by some other justification. To compel a prohibitor to restrain to do what he prohibits, there should be another prohibitor, wielding over the former. What establishes a law must be subjected to another law of a higher order, but laws of a lower order, the laws it establishes, are not applicable to it.

Taking on this line, we have to recognize that there must be objects which should be either "be or not be" and objects of which we cannot say that they can either be or not be. Thus we have "existence" of two different sorts: things which can exist or not and things whose existence is of some other sort.

The solution which is based on two "strata" of *being* (which yet has avoided somehow being regressive) is a metaphysical solution. Metaphysics, generally speaking, is what may aim to give decisions to problems of any degree of generality. In particular, a contradiction might be solved by providing another sort of existence, the one which allows contradictions.

Yet we have to reject the metaphysical solution. The reason is that it is false, not that it is properly metaphysical.

Objects which are subjected to the law of contradiction and objects which are subjected to laws of a higher order; and laws of the kind of the law of contradiction and laws of a higher order can be represented by nothing but concepts or terms which differ one from another, they are nothing but the terms A B C D ....Thus all we have to do is to add the terms with other modes of connection keeping within distinctness, namely the terms 0 and X, and then to conclude (0 A B C D....X P) from (0 A B C D....X), thus yielding the same paradox which we were trying to avoid. (Besides, to break non-contradiction means to break distinctness).

The Ontological Solution

On one hand we have language that generates paradoxes. On the other hand we have the paradox of language itself. Confronted with this dilemma, what are we to do if we do not really want to yield to the necessity of an insane and illogical choice between the absurdities of language and the absurdity of using language – the choice which could not solve anything?

All we are to do is to leave language.

We should leave language as the single subject of our speculations and to see whether there can be something extra-linguistic in them (or in their background).

We define the language of the distinct terms as the language where a term may be iterated but having been iterated, it must change its meaning. When A is iterated: A A, then A means what A means and A, which is iterated, means what A, which is not iterated, does not mean – A A designates what A does not designate.

We may say that, in a sense, language is such that it is not able to designate something which is iterated (and if we cannot express something that is iterated with language, it is senseless to speak about the existence of that). And that is really what we meant. We made an assumption that terms of language were distinct, which implied that language had no means to designate something that was *iterated*, no matter whether it existed or not.

But we may also say that we can assume that language is such that it is able to designate something which is iterated just because *there is really nothing that is iterated*. Language is such that iterations have other meaning than what is iterated because the world is such that it can stand no Iterations. Language may be assumed to have no iterations because the world may not have any Iterations.

Instead of assuming that language consists of the distinct terms, we assume that the world consists of distinct entities. The expression "distinct entity" is tautological; "entity" means a distinct, separate thing, but we construe this as emphasizing. By mentioning of distinct entities we mean that the characteristic of the entities is that they cannot repeat. This is the world of no recurrences. Any recurrence or repetition is nevertheless a new entity. That is, repetitions are yet distinct from what is repeated. Repeated or would-be the same entities are yet distinct.

The subject distinguishes between distinct, different and the same, identical. But the world – i.e. the external world, that which is deemed "objective", independent of the subject's will or the subject's perception – is blind to this. In the world all entities are distinct. A and A in the world are always distinct, while the subject in order to say they are distinct must connect distinctions: A(B) and A(C). And we say the same if we say that the subject is not keen enough to see immediately that A and A are distinct, as perhaps it really is.

The "level" of the world is the "level" of the uniformity of distinctness – entities are uniform only in the sense that they are distinct. Only their variety is unvarying in them. If there is some Sameness in them, this Sameness derives from the fact that an entity is different from all the others (this fact needs no testing in the world, as it is done in language, generating numbers). Sameness appears in this world only as distinctness. If we picture the entities of the world as

A B C D E F G....

then the alternative might be visualized as

A B C C E F G G H....

The difference between the former and the latter picture is that in the latter sameness is not "leveled" to all distinct entities whatever – sameness is not in distinctness, but sameness in the latter picture may be the sameness of C and C, or the sameness of G and G etc.... Language reaches this level with numbers, sets (understood as containing distinct members) and logic.

The general and the particular, a law and its particular case, a proposition and any of its possible variables are correspondingly equal, for they are nothing but distinct entities.

That one thing, one entity, is distinct from another, taken as the only reliable assertion to be said on an entity, seems to be a poor characteristic. This is poor, since this is the common property of things. Distinctness of an entity excludes all other possible definitions of the kind. The general characteristic of distinctness is the exhaustive general characteristic for all entities.

For suppose we give another definition for all entities. But knowing that all entities must be distinct from each other, we should conclude that this definition can hold only for one of the entities or at least for some of them.

To be distinct is the definition of every thing. All other possible definitions

The Ontological Solution   97

are particular. We may say, in a sense, that to be means to be distinct. Until we can say how something is distinct from others, we cannot establish its existence. A definition of a thing is an account of its characteristic features, the features which summingly point out how the defined thing differs from other things. The necessity to identify, when establishing existence of a thing, comes from the fact that a thing may exist only as different from other things – its existence consists in being distinct.

If we have A and A instead of A, then we are to know why A and A are different. For in the world A and A are different only because they are A and A, but not A.

Things are distinct simply because this is the way they exist. Difference from anything (or from everything) implies existence of what is different from anything else. Thus this concept of existence implies that something cannot exist alone. To exist and not have something in co-existence is nonsensical.

If to be distinct is to exist, then how this existence can be characterized except as consisting of distinct entities? Those must be *any* characteristics. If entities of the world are distinct i.e. if everything is different from everything, then nobody can say what kind of entities there can be. All that can be said is that another entity is distinct from all others. This world deprives us of the possibility to predict: prediction and what meant to be predicted must differ. The fulfillment of a law may turn out to be no its instance. A rule is not a move that the rule requires. This is the world of which everything may be said. We cannot say anything definite of all entities taken together, but this is not because the world of such entities is vague by its nature – this is by the opposite reason: the entities of the world are absolutely distinctive.

The External World

Thus we have extrapolated the idea of distinctness, which we earlier applied to language, over the external world. Instead of stating that language's Grammar is such that it requires connection of the distinct terms, we assume that the external world is such that its entities are distinct.

We have given a sketchy description of what a world it is to be if it is the world understood as consisting of distinct entities. This is the world where laws are by no means of greater importance than the phenomena they describe; the world in which we cannot be sure of anything, for our previous knowledge may be quite inapplicable to the facts coming. If it still is, we have no guarantee what it will be at the next moment or at some other space or circumstances etc.... In this kind of world the next phenomenon may totally cancel the previous one and even the expectation that if now is the one the next is to be quite another, cannot be justified. Entities are Distinct in some higher sense, we cannot conform to the fact of distinctness, we cannot Predict that. That entities are Distinct is beyond any expectations; it is what makes us feel that the world is outer, objective and independent of the subject. The world where one is necessarily different from another and the difference one might be reckoning on is not necessary may seem uncomfortable and even odd, for to have Distinctness as the single Sameness is an oddity, and what such distinctness implies may seem to be oddities too. But this world is not absurd.

To be odd, strange does not mean to be absurd. And we do not see any contradiction in the fact that the world consists of distinct entities, unlike in the case when we assume that terms of language are distinct, escaping from paradoxes.

Now we do not assume that terms of language are distinct. Now we assume that entities of the world are distinct. And, consequently, we are to construct language that pictures this world in accordance with what the world is. The distinct terms are just picturing distinct entities of the world.

Language is a part of the world, and if we construct language in the way the world is constructed, we do not arrive at any contradictions. If we know that entity A and entity A are distinct, simply because no entity can be iterated, i.e. an iteration is only able to generate another entity but not to repeat the same one; then we are to establish that in language the term A A can stand for anything but not for what the term A can stand for. Thus we exclude the possibility to mistake A A for A; and so, constructing language in the way the world is constructed, we avoid paradoxes.

Terms A B C D....represent entities of the world. They are distinct because the entities are distinct.

Besides terms A B C D.... are themselves nothing but a part of the world and as such they cannot be not distinct, i.e. they are themselves distinct entities. And, naturally, if we take them for other ones – if we consider as admitted that A A may be A, then we sooner or later lapse into contradictions.

It is the world that makes language consisting of the distinct terms. And then; if having A B C D....and adding 0 X, we deduce P, we do not deduce P from what it contains (P is P and A for any A), we do not deduce from itself what is not deducible; but what we do is concluding from the existence of distinct entities A B C D....O X that there is another distinct entity P (A B C D.... and 0 and X and P, each with its, or their, own properties).

When language is considered only in the assumption that it consists of the distinct terms, we arrive at the conclusion that language shows its own underivability, deriving that is not derivable. And that is absolutely paradoxical. When we assume that terms of language represent distinct entities of the world, we conclude – which is shown in the implication "if (0 A B C D....X) then (0 A B C D....X P)" – that distinct entities A B C D.... imply another distinct entity P (with the property "for any A, P and A is P"), of which it may be said that it cannot be explained since it explains itself (any terms of language connected to "language" are language), or it is not derivable, not deducible. That language is unexplainable, underivable in the given sense is just its distinctive feature, i.e. that which makes the entity of language be distinct among all other distinct entities. Regarded this way, our implication "if (0 A B C D....X) then (0 A B C D....X P)" brings about no contradiction.

This is what we can propose as the solution of that which we call here "the paradox of language".

And this solution is ontological. Trying to find out the solution of the paradox of language, we arrived at the ontology of distinct entities. And as the price of the solution – whether it is big or small – we have the recognition of the existence of the external world.

Realism Inferred

Why are we sure that the world is nothing but distinct entities? Is the world of distinct entities *actually* the only given real world, that which can be described only in terms of distinct entities – that which is really such; or is that a mental construction helping us to extricate from our paradoxes, just the one of the constructions that has happened to be adequate to avoid them?

The answer is that only if we could have another language, we could have another world. The logic of our conclusion that the world consists of distinct entities is a *reductio ad absurdum*. If we did not suppose that there were the external world and it had to be distinct entities, we would remain with the absurdity of the paradox of language.

The concept of the world of distinct entities is neither supposed nor assumed; distinct entities were not taken as an axiom or something so obvious that we need not even to single out as a postulate. That the world is distinct entities is a product of inference. We have to recognize that the outer world exists and that it must be necessarily consisting of nothing else but distinct entities. For, as it has been elucidated, there can be nothing extra-linguistic except for the outer world and there is nothing that, while being pictured only by language, does not generate contradictions except for the concept of the world of distinct entities. Having confronted with paradoxes which were generated in language on one side and with the paradox of language on the opposite side, we have been urged to infer that the world exists and it does exist only as distinct entities. If we were not cornered by the contradictions of language, we would have no necessity and no ground to make those ontological statements. At least we would have no logical ground.

Our *reductio ad absurdum* is in the fact that the implication "if (0 A B C D

....X), then (0 A B C D....X P)" is rendered absurd if it is not recognized that A B C D .... are entities of the real world, it is them which are distinct and terms of language are such as they ought to be in accordance with the fact that what they mean are distinct entities and terms themselves belong to those entities too.

This provides for the generation of such an entity as language – P is a consequence of A B C D.... And this means that any P is the consequence of A B C D.... In particular the consequences of A B C D....are P* and P** – in our notation, the consequences of distinct entities are language and the philosophical I.

That the world is only distinct entities implies that there necessarily should be entities which, by their very nature, cover all entities and *are* nothing but those which cover all entities whatever – "P's" are nothing but "P's and A" for any A. Language covers all entities, and it is nothing but that which covers all entities, including various meta-languages. The philosophical I of solipsism covers all entities, and it is nothing but that which does this (just as there is no consciousness without that of which it is consciousness, as phenomenology says, another reductionist doctrine).

This way we have turned the assertion that the I represents the only reliable knowledge and hence the world is nothing but a complex of my sensations, into the assertion that the world is nothing but distinct entities and hence the entity I is a consequence of the fact that the world appears itself as distinct entities – the I, in fact, is nothing but one of the entities, though one of those which may be inferred as the consequence. (Thus, what we sense are ultimately those distinct entities, whether they look similar or not).

Solipsism is a challenge – may be as a challenge it is of greater importance than Cartesianism is as an answer. And it seems that the concept of the world of distinct entities appears to be ready to accept this challenge.

Despite that the attitude to ignore the arguments of solipsism is widely spread, they are hardly so unworthy as to be ignored (if one does not replace the philosophical I of solipsism by that meant in psychology). Having found out that the I is a consequence of distinct entities, we regain the world that solipsism has made us lose. But the world we regain can only be the world of distinct entities, otherwise all previous arguments of solipsism become valid again and we are left without any objective world at all. The arguments against solipsism cannot be valid if we do not point out the cause of the solipsist conclusion (by analogy, paradoxes could not be resolved if their cause were not revealed). And it is the consequence of the concept of distinct entities which is able to present this cause. Simply, distinct entities are that which *generate* phenomena that are felt, conceived and treated as "language" or as the philosophical I.

"Fixed Points" and Physics

It is interesting to notice that entities whose way to exist is in covering all other entities – the ones we identify with fixed points of topological space – may occur in fields where they seemingly are not expected to be. That is, it seems that nature can provide us with phenomena, which we can construe to be such entities, and this may appear to be amazing enough.

It is known from the Special Relativity Theory that the speed of light is the same within any system of coordinates. We have no signal that could be more rapid than light. This means that any information can be obtained only within the adequate time-lag. If an observer wants to obtain only exact data, i.e. if he is not interested in any approximations, he must realize that construing the notions of time and space in a non-relativistic way he can never know events which happen at the moment at a certain distance from him or in a certain lapse of time. Data change as the speed of the object changes, relatively to the observer, and in accordance with the formulas of the Relativity Theory, which are made up in strict consideration of the fact that the speed of light is the same in any system of coordinates. This speed, the greatest speed, must be considered this way in all information, in all the knowledge the subject has or will ever have.

The greatest speed may be characterized in the following way: the speed of light is always equal to itself added to the speed of any body respectively to the position of the observer. We may say that the way the speed of light exists is that it remains itself when any other, less or equal, speed is added to it, i.e. if a body is moving with the speed of light, it cannot be accelerated faster, whatever momentum we are applying to it. And this essentially the same as what we may say about such entities as the philosophical I and language: the I exists with I itself together with any phenomena and language is whatever we express in language itself and we cannot know any other existence or the way of expression. No object can be registered without the subject that does it; all signs with which something is registered are those of which language consists; no data of an object can be considered without realizing that the greatest speed those data are brought with (the speed of light) is that which cannot be accelerated, remains itself and in fact the data are considered if and only if the speed is considered (of which the formulas are saying). Is the analogy a coincidence (or misconstruing) or it derives from the same principle on which the mentioned phenomena are based?

When an observer obtains data he knows quite well that the data cannot be absolutely exact, for the instruments he uses cannot be perfect enough to be able to obtain data with an arbitrary degree of precision. Moreover, the observer cannot obtain more exact data by way of enhancing the precision of his instruments to an arbitrary degree, for the measurer influences the measurements he is making; the observer's instruments should inevitably influence the data he is trying to obtain.

And this is how the indeterminacy principle is commonly formulated. That is, in short, "the observer's influence on data is necessarily held".

The fact that data are not exact and even the fact that an observer's influence can alter the data observed was well known in classical physics. But since the discoveries of Quantum Mechanics, which says that it is not possible to measure the momentum and the coordinates of a particle simultaneously, this assertion is regarded as one of the most fundamental principles of nature.

If we *juxtapose* the property of nature that instruments influence the data, as one of its fundamental principles, and the possibility to improve the instruments, we ultimately decide in favor of the principle. As well, trying to add greater speed to the body with the speed of light, we yield the speed of light. Language is anything expressed in language, the I is anything in the senses of the I – P, juxtaposed to any A, is P. (Where P may be the principle of nature that instruments influence the data, the speed of the most rapid signal, etc.; and A may be a speed less than that or equal to that, the data obtained with more precise instruments, etc.).

When asked whether these uniformities are occasional, we are inclined to answer in the negative.

For in all four cases we are confronted with the question of identification. Both making measures in the micro-world, obtaining signals from the objects, wishing thereby to have information of something; and designating things, being conscious of something; we are doing the same, we are identifying entities, distinguishing one thing among all the others. And, obviously, the act of identification is possible only if entities in principle can be distinguished, i.e. when they are distinct. And if the entities we are dealing with are distinct; then, in accordance with what was said above, there must exist the entities in question, i.e. "P"s. And having tacitly agreed that one point of space-time may be distinguished from another – i.e. that points are distinct – we are in the right to expect the possibility of existence of such entities as the relativistic speed, the indeterminacy principle (i.e. the existence of "P"s). Some would object, saying, that there is crucial difference between the laws of physics and language and that which is called the philosophical I. The former ones are corroborated by experience – thus the relativistic speed was obtained long before the theory; the latter ones can contain falsities and fantasies, things which can be neither proved nor disproved. But we insist only on the *possibility* of this kind of experience – the experience which corroborates existence of entities like "P"s (in our particular case the relativistic speed and the impossibility to get rid of the observer's influence; i.e. measuring momentum he changes the coordinates, and in reverse). If we just assume that physics is dealing with objects that can be in principle distinguished one from another, we can predict neither relativistic effects nor indeterminacy; but we can predict the existence of entities of *this kind*, of entities like "P"s, though without the slightest idea what exactly those "P"s could be (of course, this is under condition that one recognizes that the speed and the principle are among those entities: "data of arbitrary precision which are tried to avoid to be influenced are still necessarily influenced" and "an arbitrary speed added to the relativistic speed is still the relativistic speed" are both equivalent to "for any A, A and P is P").

(Perhaps, if we had not still assumed that objects of the world must be in principle distinguished one from another (the world is the world of distinct entities), but had already noticed the similarity between language and the I on one hand and the relativistic speed and indeterminacy on the other hand; then we could make conjecture (not a conclusion) that the world might be the world of distinct entities where one object are to be in principle distinguished from another, just knowing the fact of the similarity. For physics deals with the real world; and if we know that it contains entities, i.e. "P"s, which may be regarded as consequences of distinct entities; it is easier to tumble to the conjecture that it is the real world which may be consisting exclusively of distinct entities).

The ontology of distinct entities is a kind of ontology – and may be it is the single one – which is not peremptory. We are not stating straightway that the world is such and such, but firstly we are giving basis for this kind of statement. And this is not a matter of taste whether to accept that basis or not to accept. The one who wishes to reject this basis has to give his own explanations either of that which is called here the paradox of language or of contradictions which are generated by ordinary language itself. It seems that distinct entities is the "substance" of which our world is made, just as a space is made of its points (if we do imagine the entity of the world whose entities cannot be distinguished one from another (we are regarding the space as topological), this is the entity X). The concept of the distinct entity is that on which the concept of a thing of our world must be based. Thus, having the concept of the distinct entity, we need no help of the concept of the distinct term to deduce the three laws of logic – the assertions which determine the way a thing can only exist; contrary to the way we had to go above.

Heraclites' Philosophy

Suppose we have overcome all the doubts – or have not had any – and have accepted the concept of the world of distinct entities together with all that follows from the concept and all that constitutes its basis – i.e. we would not find erroneous the ideas which supported the concept. Then, were there anybody else who would accept it, or are we alone? Does it differ much from what philosophers hold or is it possible to find similar opinions?

Very soon we shall see that in order to answer this, it is most convenient for us to begin with the following citation (Popper 1963, p 11-12):

> Heraclites was the philosopher who discovered the idea of change. Down to this time, the Greek philosophers, influenced by Oriental ideas, had viewed the world as a huge edifice of which the material things were building material. It was the totality of things – the cosmos (which originally seems to have been an Oriental tent or mantle). The questions which the philosophers asked themselves were: "What stuff is the world made of?", or "How is it constructed, what is its true ground plan?" They considered philosophy, or physics (the two were indistinguishable for a long time) as the investigation of "nature", i.e. of the original material out of which this edifice, the world, had been built. As far as any processes were considered, they were thought of either as going on within the edifice, or else as constructing or maintaining it, disturbing and restoring the stability or balance of a structure which was considered to be fundamentally static. They were cyclic processes (apart from the processes connected with the origin of the edifice; the question "Who has made it?" was discussed by the Orientals, by Hesiod and by others). This very natural approach, natural even to many of us to-day, was superseded by the genius of Heraclites. The view he introduced was that there was no such edifice, no stable

structure, no cosmos. "The cosmos, at best, is like a rubbish heap scattered at random" is one of his sayings. He visualized the world not as an edifice, but rather as one colossal process; not as the sum-total of all things, but rather as the totality of all events, or changes or facts. "Everything is in flux and nothing is at rest" is the motto of his philosophy.

We have chosen this extract because of this contraposition of the very first philosophers who were actually trying to make the physical picture of the world and Heraclites views which seems to represent the starting point of philosophy as such, as that which is to be called "philosophy" proper. For this is the task of a physicist to find out behind the variety of phenomena some elements which help to answer the question how all this variety is constructed, or to what all these different and continuously changing phenomena may be reduced. It was Heraclites who proposed a purely philosophical decision: What the world really is is this variety of different phenomena itself, not some constituent elements which could be in their background. And this entails that the world is just a rubbish heap scattered at random – everything is in flux, strife, continuous change, no thing is at rest.

If we state that the world consists of distinct entities, we do not presuppose that those entities must constitute some static edifice or construction. For if we add to the concept of distinct entities the concept that each of them must be that of the construction, we do alter the concept itself, we actually mean that entities are not distinct in all senses of the word, that they are the same as the constituent parts of the edifice. But the concept admits the existence of different constructions (not necessarily contradictory or opposite, but of any kind; but not necessary of any kind).

It would be more correct to compare distinct entities with a "rubbish heap scattered at random", but it is only as correct as any comparison may be (i.e. they are such "at best"). Distinct entities cannot be determined in principle, even if they are determined as a haphazard collection. If one is necessarily distinct from another, it is something that purposely lacks any organization, except for the distinctness. While something that is scattered at random may seem to be regarded as allowing repetitions (even if it is scattered at random in order not to have repetitions, there still remains such *probability*; and the *intention itself* to scatter at random obviously clash the notion of distinct entities).

Distinct entities may be compared to a flux where nobody can enter twice. And this can be interpreted as corresponding to Heraclites' philosophy.

The philosophy which establishes the concept of the world of distinct entities is the philosophy which insists simply that one and one is not one. If we said that one and one were two, we would say too much, we would concentrate on "effect" and omit the "cause" (numbers exist because entities are different one to another). In this philosophy events do not repeat. When we say "It is the same event" (or "fact", "thing"), what we are saying is an abstraction. For we just abstract, omit some characteristics of the event. (Entities may seem the same, but to be distinct means not to exist alone – we always can find other entities to serve as distinctions of the entities which seem to be the same, to characterize them).

And in order to express the idea of this philosophy we may choose the assertion that it is impossible to enter one and the same flow twice. This sounds as a poetical form of the assertion that one and one is not one, that it is not possible to repeat the same event, etc....

We have chosen the extract cited above because of Popper's views exposed in it. He says that a very natural approach to the universe, when one asks "How is the world constructed?", "What a plan it has and what are its elements?"– the approach which is to be adopted by physicists, was superseded by Heraclites; that is, before Heraclites this approach had never appeared in philosophy. Since Heraclites physics and philosophy have become strictly separated. Thus, it may be said that in a sense together with Heraclites philosophy there appears philosophy as such.

As we have seen, the concept of the world of distinct entities seems similar to the concept which regards the world as a flux, constant change, "rubbish heap, at best". The world as a "process" may be the process consisting simply of distinguishing any entity from any other. We have asked, whether there were anyone to hold similar views as we did; and it seems that we have found those similar views, given in another form, may be intended to have more general meaning.

But it seems that we did something more than having found similar philosophical concept. We have found that in *a certain sense* the concept of distinct entities is philosophy proper – the concept of distinct entities is in a sense similar to Heraclites' philosophy and his philosophy is the one which begins philosophizing without a mixture of physics – the ends peculiar to physics were abandoned by philosophers.

The Integrated View

We have noticed the similarity between distinct entities, that is, in our symbols, A B C D..... , and "rubbish heap" or "flux" of Heraclitus. But we also have something to compare to the consequences of A B C D . . . . ., i.e. to P's, i.e. to distinct entities of some other kind than A B C D..... proper.

Thus, for Parmenides the world is only what can be described by his concept of the "whole". The world is represented by the "whole", which has no parts, no attributes, it is infinite, it is perfect, and so forth. It seems that the "whole" is such a concept, such an entity, which must characterize what contains all, what need not and cannot be completed. Suppose we designate that entity P; then if at all there is anything to characterize P, and if we characterize it, we always yield P again - for any A, P and A is P. It seems that "for any A, P and A is P" is a scheme for such concepts as the "whole". The "whole" is what must have its own characteristics "in whole".

Suppose one's position consists in questioning any knowledge. He is successfully arguing with anyone who claims to know what is good, what is truth, etc. What must his own knowledge be? He deems his knowledge reliable since while others think that they know something, he neither knows anything nor thinks that he knows; that is, all he knows is that he knows nothing. And this is the only knowledge he would not question - otherwise his position of questioning could be invalidated. Thus, within his position, his knowledge (he knows that he knows nothing) - let us call it P, having set beside any knowledge of truth, good, etc., which he keeps to question - let us call any of it "A" - will always supersede the knowledge he questions - simply because his knowledge is unquestionable (for any A, A and P is P). This unquestionable knowledge always remains the most reliable.

Suppose now someone thinks of the problem of being (or existence). He is trying to find out what it means to exist: that what we can say it exists without doubt or the risk of making a mistake? He concludes that the most reliable is thinking itself -"I think, then I exist". Unlike something which is supposed as being or as a certain essence of all that exists - the essence of the kind that could be asserted in metaphysics - my thinking cannot arise any doubts of its reality. That I think (P) and whatever I think being is (A) is yet no more than that I think (P).

Is this interpretation of the famous and easily recognizable doctrines too far-fetched, made up with intention to fit the maintained conception, or we may say that philosophical doctrines (or certain philosophical doctrines) are made up unintentionally according to a certain pattern or "algorithm" which the conception must somehow provide?

Suppose we reject that this interpretation is far-fetched and accept the latter view. In that case, what we do explicitly hold?

If the world is distinct entities, then a philosophy must be a way to say that. Its conceptions must be similar to this conception. An example of it is the philosophy of Heraclitus. The conceptions of a philosophy may not approach in any way to the conception of distinct entities, but they may approach to the consequence of this conception. A philosophy may contain a conception which is subjected to the scheme "for any A, A and P is P". A philosophy may not establish in this or that way the existence of A B C D... , but it may establish the existence of some P, for which for any A B C ..(or A or B or C...) and P is always P.

If in a philosophy the conception P is found (if we find a concept which yields itself when connected to any other concept), then this means that this conception cannot be predicated about, i.e. whatever we would assert about that, generally speaking, this could be only tantamount to that itself, i.e. to that of which it is asserted.

If the world is distinct entities, to philosophize must mean to clarify this fact. But philosophy often chooses conceptions which fit P in the scheme "for any A, A and P is P". For P cannot be predicated. The entities "P" are to remain as they are, they cannot be altered. Using traditional philosophical terminology (maybe in somewhat warped way), we may say that predicating on this kind of entities can be only *analytic*; i.e. making statements on those entities, we could not add to our knowledge of them; but our use of the word "analytic" is evidently wider than traditional - whatever we know, those entities are as they are, just as it is with the real things.

Thus, suppose our knowledge is being enriched with more and more laws which we discover in nature, but whatever laws we discovered, all of them would exist in our pure reason. The world of noumena (things in themselves) is beyond our cognition and whatever the natural laws are, all we can yield is that our cognition is limited by noumena (the world of noumena (P) remains despite any progress of cognition (A)).

Or, no matter which psychological acts go with perception of something or conception of something (A's), all that is reduced to phenomena (P), those which exist in consciousness and without which it is senseless to say about "consciousness" or something conscious.

Or, philosophy may give various solutions to philosophical problems. There are many answers to the questions "What is the truth?", "What is being?", "What is cognition?" etc... But better than giving those various answers (A's), the existence is being clarified by that act of putting questions itself (P).

That itself that the existence may be represented as a certain unity (dialectically developed from some being or established straightaway as that unity) may be construed as "whatever phenomena there are, (A's), there remains ultimately only that unity (P)".

Phenomena of the world may be nothing but a deceptive illusion (A's) (as it is in Indian philosophy) and the Will (P), i.e. not that which is contained in representation, i.e. in these illusory phenomena, but rather that which cannot be expressed in words and which therefore is not illusory unlike the phenomena are.

Various doctrines (A's) there were made (and various doctrines there are made) which teach what it means to exist. But the question (or the task) is to elucidate the existence itself (P) - rather straightaway, describing acts and circumstances of those who exist.

If it is not far-fetched that the pattern "for any A, A and P is P" is applicable or is the basis for each of the above listed conceptions, then it seems that some conceptions are made according to one and the same pattern. And the conceptions having been regarded are often deemed crucial as to the development of philosophy. But the one who is going to assert this should be cautious. For this pattern is obviously of the kind that it might be applicable for too large number of things.

The idea that philosophical systems are to be constructed according to a single paradigm seems attractive; it could have justified the tendency of various philosophical doctrines (some say mostly Western ones or only "continental") toward the integrated view. Versus this idea there is the impediment of traditional approach to philosophy as to the science without a method, the approach which estimates the value of a philosophy in its originality. Besides, there are different exegeses for one and the same philosophical system. If one recognized that a philosophy was constructed in accordance with the paradigm, another might not do.

But exegeses are not what exist with a philosophy. Any exegesis of a philosophy has its own idea out of the philosophy, according to which it treats this philosophy. And the idea that some (or many, or all) philosophical systems are done according to the pattern "for any A, A and P is P" might itself serve for exegesis of many systems (not only those which were regarded).

The Copenhagen Interpretation

Someone contemplating on "real", physical things may at the very first glance decide that physical bodies remain physical bodies and we cannot say that they are of those entities which cannot repeat, which we cannot perceive as the same at certain moments of time in certain places.

But actually this is a physical (or even pre-physical) pre-conception. It is an abstraction to state that there are certain "physical bodies"; actually, physics deals with data. All existing physical bodies are concrete; they have their coordinates, properties, characteristics. And, when taking measurements of an object, we cannot get twice one and the same data of the object. If we are doing two or more measurements, we are yielding two or more different sets of data; when we measure an object once, we yield data of the first measurement and we measure the object twice, we yield data of the second measurement etc. But we decide on the existence of a body using those measurements.

Thus, we state that the glass of water that we are looking at now is the same glass of water that we looked at an hour earlier, despite that we have measured that such-and-such quantity of molecules have evaporated. But we do not state that particles after annihilation are just another form of those which were before their annihilation – they are other particles. It does not matter what we call "this physical body" and what we call "another physical body", what matters is what data we obtain: particles with such-and-such characteristics, that volume of liquid, etc. But it is entirely impossible to repeat measurements of an object. Even in the most static case, intentionally given, the time-coordinate will change. And it is impossible to conclude that a phenomenon repeats without making *different*, other observations.

All we know about the physical world are our data of facts. We obtain them by observations, doing measurements. And it does not require any proof that we register a phenomenon making one observation (or measuring) and we register the phenomenon twice only making the second observation etc. We establish the existence of a fact on the basis of such-and-such observations (or measurements) done under such-and-such circumstances. If we want to corroborate the existence of a fact (or to reject the assertion of its existence) we are to do other observations (maybe of similar kind) in other (maybe in similar) circumstances. The fact may happen to be corroborated or not by another observation, and even if it is corroborated, it is done by another observation, not that through which we have established the existence of the fact firstly. The fact may be deemed (or not) to remain the same, but the observations are different each time. Since the observations are the only basis on which we may establish the existence of the fact, we may say that when we refer to facts, we refer to the observations and in reverse. Whenever we mean a fact, we mean different instances of its observations (or an observation of it, if it is the single instance).

The picture of the physical world which says that all we know is our data of facts obtained by observations which, no matter whether on a single fact or several facts, cannot *repeat* is the picture which is much nearer to the truth than any presuppositions about physical bodies. Besides, this picture corresponds to the idea that the world is distinct entities. Even if facts are similar, observations, which may be only different, may serve as distinctions to them – thus, all the data we can obtain may be only distinct.

If the facts observed turn out to be different, then this means that we know that just observing different objects or by different characteristics of objects observed. And if the observed fact is the same, this means that we can distinguish the fact by different observations of it. Otherwise, we could not determine that the fact observed is the same.

In micro-physics it is not always possible to tell whether the same particle has been observed or not, and obtaining one characteristic we are losing another – knowing momentum, it is not possible to learn the position, and knowing position we cannot learn momentum. Just by measuring a particle we disturb it by – learning position we are giving momentum or having the momentum measured we lose the position. But if we do not observe the same object and the characteristics may not be those we wish to obtain, can we nevertheless say that we are able to *distinguish* facts? By observing, we are distinguishing one object from another, obtaining characteristics, which help to identify objects. Thus, we have data of which may be said that they are the series that represent distinct entities. The same object under different observations gains corresponding characteristics – say of some other time of observation – and this provides its sameness, because the observations are showing no changing except for different time. Different objects are given in data giving different characteristics of the objects as the different ones. But how can one distinguish objects one from another if observations must change the characteristics with whose help objects are to be distinguished?

In other words, could we be in the right to explain the picture in terms of the concept of distinct entities if the observations themselves alter what makes objects be distinct, namely the distinctions themselves, in particular position and momentum?

In that case, we may say that we are able to describe events only as we are making observations, but we are not able to describe events between two observations. All that we can say is what happens while we observe an event but we cannot say what happens while we *do not* observe. The notion of event has any meaning only if we talk of an event as of what we observe. Observations change the reality and our knowledge cannot spread over the span or distance between them.

It follows from this that if observations change events this should guarantee that events of any series of observations are to be distinct, one member of the series from another. If observations change the reality, there can be, in general sense, no same events to be observed.

Suppose we take measurements and state as the result of the measurement that the event A takes place. But the measuring devices must influence what we have measured. Thus, if we have established that the event A takes place, we must expect that as a result of the subsequent influence, the event A is no longer possible – there should be a different event if we make another measurement.

Thus, in the macro-world the distinctness of data we obtain is provided by different characteristics of the events described, whether it is spacio-temporial characteristics or characteristics of the objects; but after a certain threshold, namely in the scale of the measurements restricted by the quantum of action, the distinctness of events is provided by the observations themselves.

If we can observe the objective world distinguishing objects one from another by checking their different characteristics, we do all we ought to do and able to do in the world of distinct entities to describe this world as it only should be and is able to be described. But if our observations are becoming so precise that we cannot help but to disturb the observed objects, we can distinguish events by virtue of the very change brought by our observations to the objects – once we have changed something obtaining data, this means that we cannot, generally, repeat it. Thus in this case, too, all that we are doing is describing *distinct* events, the ones of the single kind the world can give us to perceive.

As for the picture of the world given by the concept of distinct entities, there can be no puzzle, no predicament, and by far no contradiction in the assertion that making changes in the data by observations, we are unable to tell what "happens between" the two observations that have been made; for the concept of such a world do not require the existence any "course of events" except for the series of events which are distinct from each other, no matter whether they are contingent or subjected to a law, what seems to be sufficient is that a definitely coherent way to establish their distinctness is therefore given.

The view that, roughly speaking, it is superfluous to put questions on what happens between the two events observed is known in Quantum Theory as the

Copenhagen Interpretation. In this interpretation it is particularly emphasized that any attempt to find a description of what happens between two observations would lead to contradictions. The initial experimental situation in Quantum Mechanics is translated into a probability function and the concept of the probability function does not allow such descriptions. The observation itself changes the function discontinuously, making speak about "quantum jump". The Copenhagen Interpretation excludes any construing of the experimental situations that would allow a description of what happens with something which we do not observe. This interpretation rejects the idea of certain "hidden parameters" which would be able to find a way to discover and explain the events in "absence" of the observer. This interpretation states that it is in principal, impossible for such "events", to appear in the micro-world.

The picture of the world opposing this interpretation presupposes that objects are independent of the observer and our knowledge of events must not be restricted to the probability – even if observations disturb the situation, the "real" course of events should be as determinate in the predictions as it is in the macro-world – it should not be indeterminate in principle. According to this picture the situation with the course of events in the macro-world presents a general law, though we cannot fully know it in the micro-world because of our observations' interference.

Another approach which differs from the Copenhagen Interpretation – it should be noticed that the Copenhagen interpretation is accepted by the great majority of physicists – is the revision of the classical logic. Thus, referring to some experimental results, in the Quantum Logic the classical law of distribution does not hold. The bivalence of the classical logic (the presence of the assertion of the excluded middle) in such revisions may also be questioned – the condition of a particle out of observations may be regarded neither as that which can be denied nor as that which can be corroborated, but as that which is "undecidable". Among the adherents of the revision of logic there may be not only whose who just do not follow the materialistic views that that which happens between observations is not senseless to speak about, but also those who could deny any philosophical realism at all.

For the construing of the experimental situations given by the Copenhagen Interpretation there is obviously no necessity in the revision of logic – this interpretation gives a simpler solution than any such revision. As for the concept of distinct entities, it may be said that its understanding of the "course of events" – the idea that all that is to be required is their distinctness – corresponds to the understanding which is in the basis of the interpretation; *but* this understanding (the one given by the concept of distinct entities) is laid on the same basis as the laws of classical logic.

Before attaining the result that the world is distinct entities we had to recognize that the notion of distinctness proper could be formulated in the same way as the three laws of logic could be done. The notion of distinctness is the basis which allows for the understanding of what a course of events distinct entities provide. Changes of events by the observations are within the idea of this course of events. This gives ground neither for questioning bivalence (i. e. to have doubts about the validity of the law of the excluded middle) nor for restricting the notion of the grammatical connection which is actually proposed by the Quantum Logic (the notion of the grammatical connection is so loose because the notion of distinctness is so strict – to restrict the former is to undermine indirectly or to doubt the latter).

The treatment of the experimental results in micro-physics which is given in the Copenhagen Interpretation looks like a good illustration of the concept of distinct entities – changes in the picture of events brought by the observations of events themselves *guarantee* their distinctness (the situation is reverse to that with the ancient physics mentioned above: the philosophy of constant change is presented (in Popper's construing) as the opposition to the physics of those times whose conceptions were of "hierarchical" nature).

Systems of Distinctions

But it seems that the picture of the physical world where different observations serve as distinctions of similar facts may be applied both in case when we regard the world as distinct entities and in case when we admit existing of entities in the world which are distinct and entities which are similar.

In other words, we could not necessarily assert that the world was distinct entities; and in case the facts happened to be similar, we could distinguish them by the time (or other coordinate or circumstances) when the observations of them had been done. If we did this, we would have a unique system of distinctions.

But, *recognizing* that the world is distinct entities; can we be sure that any system of distinctions – this one in particular – could be valid forever? Can we be sure that this system of distinctions works for the next instance?

If we do assume that the world is distinct entities, we cannot be sure that the single system of distinctions is always valid. We can say that each application of a certain system of distinctions satisfies the assumption, but we cannot say that instances are distinct due to a certain system of distinctions. For we have assumed that they are distinct as they are and it cannot depend on any such system. That is, we are to admit that even if a system breaks down, instances must be nevertheless distinct – due to another such system or just despite that one.

To say that entities are distinct means to guarantee that one entity must be distinct from another. And to say that entities are distinct means not to guarantee that *any* system which helps to distinguish entities can be always valid.

The latter assertion immediately follows from the necessity that entities are distinct. If we admitted that entities might be distinct and might not be, we then had to admit that that which allowed us to distinguish entities could not fail. But if entities are distinct, any next entity (if there is at all) is distinct to all the previous; and that which helps to distinguish entities is no exception – the next system of distinctions (if there is at all) must be distinct from the previous one.

Laws and Distinctions

The fact that a system of distinctions is not guaranteed to be hold is fraught with consequences.

For let us suppose that N is a series of similar facts, â is a system of distinctions. Suppose N(â) is the application of this system to the facts of the kind. But, as we have mentioned, the constancy of â is not guaranteed – it is not guaranteed that â is always that which makes distinguish the instances of N. Were there any other system of distinctions in place of â, its constant validity had not been guaranteed too.

But if there is no guarantee that â is valid, then there should be no guarantee that N is similar instances; i.e. if â cannot distinguish instances of N, then N *themselves* must be distinct (that is, no system of distinctions must be needed to distinguish them one from another, they must not be similar).

Thus, similar instances of facts may be established as appearance of a law. But from the above said it follows that if N are those facts (N is a law) and there is no such B which is a guaranteed system of distinctions for N, i.e. N(â), then the fulfillment of the law is not guaranteed. And this holds for any facts (in particular for those of which we say that they are corroborating a law) – this holds for any law.

We have found out that the validity which we can ascribe to laws of nature must be restricted by the concept of distinct entities.

What we have actually said is that validity of natural laws cannot be guaranteed, since in the world of distinct entities validity of any system of distinctions cannot be guaranteed.

Suppose we have a number of objects. Those objects are subjected to a law. This means that each of the objects have a property (or some) which is similar in all the objects. This property, common to all the objects, is the one which the law covers, and mentions. Properties by which objects differ are the basis for a system of distinctions. Suppose such a system is established: we have selected properties with whose help we distinguish one object from another – this system constitutes of a number of such properties. That this system of distinctions cannot be guaranteed for further objects means that the latter may not have the property which was common for the previous number of objects. Considering this property we yield another system of distinctions.

Suppose now for the sake of example that there are some swans. Their common property is that they are white (suppose their property to be white is a certain "biological law") – the properties to serve as distinctions are, say, age and the length of neck. But since those properties as the system of distinctions are not guaranteed for further number of swans, other properties may be added to serve as another system of distinctions. For instance, the color black may be added to discern a swan of black color but with the same length of the neck as a white swan, or to discern a swan of black color but of the same age as a swan of white color etc....

What we have actually said is that no property is guaranteed against being in a system of distinctions.

Skepticism

It is easy to see that what is exposed above is something like a version of skepticism.

Philosophical skepticism (in its Humean version) says that if a phenomenon has taken place before, it does not mean that it will take place in the future. If we are watching something constantly iterating, it does not mean that we shall observe it the next time, it may cease to appear. And if our observations are corroborating a natural law, we must realize that the law can be not valid, for further observations may not corroborate it. We have no guarantee that any iterations, no matter how long they stay, will continue forever. Although all our laws are based on the belief that it will. When we establish a law, we mean that something necessarily happens, but actually we can guarantee only that it has happened but we cannot guarantee that it will happen, not even the next moment.

The supposition that if something used to occur it may not occur in the future seems obvious and is of the kind which cannot be rejected on reasonable grounds. But this makes us doubtful concerning unobjectionable universality of natural laws.

As the skeptical motto says, if the sun rises every day, it does not mean that the sun will rise to-morrow. Or if the law of gravitation has held, it does not mean that it will hold.

Skepticism – i.e. Humean skepticism – concludes that if it is so, if the universality of laws of nature cannot take place for the reason that no further iterations of a phenomenon can be guaranteed; then all our knowledge – i.e. a system or collection of general and necessary statements – is based on associations – all that we do is just mentally associating similar facts – or just acquiring habits to consider them similar.

This skepticism says outright that iterations are not guaranteed, i.e. we cannot guarantee that a natural law is always corroborated by further instances of it. But as to the version of skepticism exposed above, it says firstly that no system of distinctions can be guaranteed to apply to all objects; then it says that since the application of any system is not guaranteed, any property of an object may be a distinction, i.e. the property of which a law defines may turn out to be not common to all objects but may turn out to be among the properties which help to distinguish one object from another.

This means that Humean skepticism may be regarded as deduced from the concept that the world is distinct entities.

Since any entity is guaranteed to be distinct from another, the entity which provides that we could discern entities – a system of distinctions – cannot be guaranteed to be one and the same. Thus, properties of objects which seem to be the same for all (or a number) of objects cannot be guaranteed to be so – no property can be counted not to be able to become a distinction. Hence no natural law can be counted to be ever valid – properties of which natural laws say are not guaranteed to maintain always and universally (e.g. the property of physical objects of conservation of energy, charge, etc.; the property of gravitation according to such and such formulas, to have such and such constants, etc.).

This looks like a more complex exposition of a skeptical view on natural laws than the skepticism proper gives. Actually skeptical attitude toward the laws of nature is a consequence of the assertion that the world is nothing but distinct entities. If we assume the latter, we necessarily have to assume the skeptical views on the human understanding of nature.

Skepticism of another Form

Skepticism of our time extends not only over laws of nature. It seems normal to be skeptical toward what is not subjected to our will, toward what we cannot rule or influence. Modern skepticism (or one of the forms of modern skepticism) extends over that which may be established by human being, over what he can control, i.e. over rules.

According to S.Kripke (1982), who upholds the skepticism on rules, this kind of skepticism was invented by Wittgenstein.

That is how the question was primarily posed by Wittgenstein. No course of action could be determined by a rule, because every course of action can be made out to accord with the rule. So if everything can be made out to accord with the rule, then it also can be made out to conflict with it. This way we could yield neither concurrence with the rule nor divergence from the rule. And this is not the question of interpretation.

Wittgenstein implies that there is something in obeying the rule or going against it that is beyond interpretation (in Kripke 1982 p.13): "Interpretations by themselves do not determine meaning.... any interpretation still hangs in the air along with what it interprets and cannot give it any support."

Starting from this, and keeping referring to many other places in Wittgenstein's later writings (most of all in "Philosophical Investigations"), Kripke comes to the conclusion about Wittgenstein's doubts that any general rule logically entails any its separate instance to be fulfilled. In other words, as to Kripke (or, if one prefers, as to what he made more explicit in Wittgenstein), this way of grasping the rule that is expressed in obeying it or going against it and that is not an interpretation is, in fact, the implication that there is no logical entailment of a rule upon its own instances. (As he put it, that is what struck him in Wittgenstein). He develops this skeptical argument (1982 p.8) instantiating in great part in the area of arithmetic, in particular, in the function of addition. Since the argument, as it is, sounds highly bizarre, we are giving it in a long extract in order to keep it within its own context sufficiently long (besides we suppose that it gives the sensation which the picture of the world of distinct entities must give, the sensation of constant change or unreliability, for which the subject often cannot find no plausible ground).

> Let me suppose, for example, that "68+57" is a computation that I have never performed before. Since I have performed – even silently to myself, let alone in my publicly observable behavior – only finitely many computations in the past, such an example surely exists. In fact, the same finitude guarantees that there is an example exceeding, in both its arguments, all previous computations. I shall assume in what follows that "68+57" serves for this purpose as well.
>
> I perform the computation, obtaining of course, the answer "125". I am confident, perhaps after checking my work, that 125 is the correct answer. It is correct both in arithmetical sense that 125 is the sum of 68 and 57, and in the metalinguistic sense that "plus", as I intended to use that word in the past, denoted a function which, when applied to the numbers I called 68 and 57, yield the value 125. Now suppose I encounter a bizarre sceptic. This sceptic questions my certainty about my answer, in what I just called "metalinguistic" sense. Perhaps, he suggests, as I need the term "plus" in the past, the answer I intended for "68+57" should have been "5". Of course the sceptic suggestion might be that the challenger should go back to school and learn to add. Let the challenger, however, continue. After all, he says, if I am now so confident that, as I used the symbol "+", my intention was that "68+57" should turn out to denote 125, this cannot be because I explicitly gave myself instructions that 125 is the result of performing the addition in this particular instance. By hypothesis, I did no such thing. But of course the idea is that in this new instance,! should apply the very same function or rule that I applied so many times in the past. But who is to say what function this was? In the past I gave myself only a finite number of examples instantiating this function. All, we have supposed, involved numbers smaller than 57. So perhaps in the past I used "plus" and "+" to denote a function which I will call "quus" and symbolise by (+). It is defined by
> x (+) y = x (+) y, if x,y<57
> =5 otherwise.
> Who is to say that this is not the function I previously meant by "+"?

The argument runs that what the sceptic doubts is whether the past cases justify the answer "125" rather than "5". He puts the challenge in terms of his skeptical hypothesis about a change in the usage. Maybe when the term "plus" is applied in the past for, say, some hundred times it always meant "quus": by his hypothesis there were explicit directions that were incompatible with such a supposition.

So it is no mathematical error, as it might be looked at the very first glance, but a justified way of reasoning from the logical point of view (1982): "Ridiculous and fantastic though it is, the sceptic's hypothesis is not logically impossible". The application of similar reasoning is not restricted to the area of mathematical rules and not even to rules properly. They may be applicable as large as they concern any sample or pattern.

Thus, if it is supposed that all we need to do to determine our use of the word "green" is to have an image, a sample, of green that is bring to mind whenever the word is applied in the future to a new object, will the skeptical problem hold? But perhaps by "green" in the past it was meant grue, and the color image indeed was grue, it was meant to direct to apply the word "green" to grue objects always. It may be supposed that in the past "green" was to apply to all and only those things "of the same color" as sample. The sceptic can reinterpret "same color" as same schmolor, where things have the same schmolor.

The skeptic can always change "green" for "grue" and "color" for "schmolor", so that we cannot refute his argument referring to a rule of a more general order. Eventually the process should end, however (1982 p.17):

> How can I justify my present application of such a rule, when sceptic could easily interpret it so as to yield any of an indefinite number of other results? It seems that my application of it is an unjustified stab in the dark. I apply the rule blindly.

Suppose we produce addition of 68 and 57 a definite number of times. We know that we have done this N times, i.e. we can assign a number to each of the instances of the addition. This may be our system of distinctions (it might have been any other as well). Naturally, the instances are entities, and hence it is not guaranteed that the system of distinctions we have chosen (i.e. the counting) are to be the single possible system. In particular, the next instance may be distinguished from the others by having "quus" instead of "plus", i.e. the instance "68 plus 57" (with a certain number assigned or any other distinction) may be followed by "68 quus 57". In other words, different instances of a rule may be different at the price of changing the very rule, for to establish that entities are distinct means to establish the impossibility of systematic distinction.

"Green" may be changed in the next instance for "grue" and "color" may be for any reason, by virtue of following or resisting any circumstances, changed for "schmolor", whatever it may mean. The distinct terms of language are Distinct in some higher sense. This "Distinctness" must surpass any uniformity of the rule following. The distinctions of the instances of the rule may not be the distinctions in *general sense,* in general sense there may be *any* system of distinctions – the requirement of the distinctness may be fulfilled in any way.

Very often skeptical arguments are used to oppose the concept of the philosophical realism (though, on the other hand, the concept of realism of distinct entities is somewhat different from that which is usually understood as "realism" in current philosophical writings). Nevertheless, we see that the possibility of the appearance of both concepts of skepticism – that of the natural laws and the one that has been just regarded – can be explained in the same way. Both of them are deduced from the concept of the world as distinct entities which cannot guarantee a constant system of distinctions.

Falsifiability

Suppose a researcher has a hypothesis, let us call it *a*. In order to remain to be a statement of language (a true statement, that which is not to be cancelled and forgotten and that which is to be preserved in language as necessary to consider) the hypothesis must be corroborated by experience, and must be connected (compared) with data. (We are calling "term" what may be a statement because this is a usual way to coin terms – a phenomenon which is called by a term may be described by a statement or some). The hypothesis consists in assertion that something has the property *a*. Suppose the researcher has an instrument which if arranged in according way allows him to obtain the data indicating that the studied phenomenon has this or that property: when arranged in the position *a'*, it allows him (or not) to obtain the property *a*; when arranged in the position *b'*, the instrument may give the property which may be correspondingly called *b* (or it may not give something of the kind) – changing of the position involves possible change of the property (if there can be such).

The researcher, adhering to the view that the phenomenon always has the property *a* (his hypothesis), adjusts the instrument and corroborates his hypothesis having obtained *a*. To be sure he repeats his experiment and the truth of the property *a* has been corroborated. Should he continue to observe the phenomenon in the position of the instrument *a'*, obtaining that the hypothesis is true (obtaining *a* at the time (or place or whatever) x – thus yielding a^x, obtaining *a* at the time y – thus yielding a^y and so on); or he should arrange his instrument confronting the possibility to obtain *b* instead of *a* (in the position which is supposed to be in accordance with *b*, i.e. *b'*) or *c* instead of *a*, etc.?

Suppose he recognizes that language has the Grammar in the sense meant above (he considers, in particular, that *aa* must be anything but *a*).

Considering that and the fact that his instrument is in the position a', his speculations may be the following: "I have the task to corroborate a. To corroborate means in language to connect grammatically to terms which express the data. Since I am to consider the Grammar of language, I should not pursue to make iterations of a (to keep obtaining data in the position of a'), iterations can only remove the term out of language; that is, remaining in the position a', I cannot corroborate a. If I did yet pursue to obtain the data in the position a', I would show only – since iterations in strict sense; $a, a, a,..$ must be out of the language with the Grammar – that a exists in different moments of time (space, order, etc): $a^x, a^y, ...$, which may be said of any data: a, b, c, etc. Those terms satisfy the requirement of the Grammar, *generally*, (unlike $aaaa....$); but in the *particular* case I do not satisfy this requirement. The Grammar says "aa is *anything* but a", not some particular b, c, or $^{x, y, z...}$ Thus, since I have other possibilities than the position a', in order to satisfy the requirement "aa is *anything* but a", I should set the instrument into the position b', even at the risk that the hypothesis a may turn out to be false, but only this way I am within the task and within the Grammar".

Experiments testing a hypothesis must be carried out so that the results contradictory to the hypothesis must be possible to be received. And hypotheses must be devised so that such experiments may be carried out. Iteration of the hypothesis's assertion in the experiments (i.e. assertions based simply on the iterated events) does not lead to the right conclusion, for iterations in the Grammar of language are substituted (e.g. aa for c) or altered (e.g. aa for aa^x). In the language with the Grammar iterations may be avoided in *any* way, iterated events corresponding to the hypothesis and distinguished by marks of, say, time, may be well replaced by event contradictory to the hypothesis – aa is *anything* but a. Thus a hypothesis is to be considered corroborated when there are no events contradictory to the hypothesis, but not when simply there are events corresponding to the hypothesis. To remain in language a term must be distinct from others, so the researcher must try to obtain b after a, but not a after a.

In other words, hypotheses must be falsified. And we have come to this conclusion *purely* in terms of the Grammar of language. Hypotheses are to be falsified because language has the Grammar; and having that, it is to alter or replace iterations no matter in *what way* and we should not know beforehand in *what way*.

Although our example and our approach to the theory of falsifiability are oversimplified, they seem to reflect the gist of the matter – the theory itself is more complex.

The Grammar and the Grammar

Evidently, we have succeeded in the explication of falsifiability in terms of the concept of the distinct terms because the concept of falsifiability considers *directly* the Humean skepticism, which is not the case with verifiability and confirmation. Skepticism is intrinsic to the concept of falsifiability. To say that hypotheses must be falsified – i.e. in order to establish the truth of a hypothesis we should prove that there are no experimental data to refute it, instead of proving that there are the experimental data to verify it – means to imply that the iterations of a phenomenon cannot serve as a basis for the conclusions of its universality and necessity, i.e. no quantity of iterations could guarantee further iterations. In the language of distinct terms (which is a part of the world of distinct entities) no iteration can mean the same as its initial notion does – what only can be *guaranteed* is their distinctness, but not the way how to distinguish them (AA may mean anything not A). This makes the distinct terms be the common background that allows presenting falsifiability and skepticism in the *same terms*. We now have all to draw the "line of demarcation" between the Grammar in the sense of the word we apply and in the usual sense of the word. Namely, we may determine the place of the Grammar of language as distinct terms and, on the other hand, the "universal grammar". The universal grammar is a system of rules which speakers of all natural languages subconsciously follow – roughly speaking, the same rules are intrinsic to all natural languages. Any natural language is constructed according to the same rules – there is a single set of "structures", "theories" and "parameters" to describe any language. Those rules have no arbitrary character. We cannot imagine them and then just care about abiding them, while knowing that there could be other such rules. In a language, it seems, there can be no grammatical rule, which would not lie within the general patterns, or general rules necessary for all natural languages out of the patterns. Those patterns are innate; language bearers speak language since they bear such patterns.

Those rules are revealed empirically. Such a rule having been established as valid for all languages is to be empirically tested. A universal rule encountering no counterexamples is to be valid, otherwise it is not. The universal grammar is recognized to be falsifiable.

The uniformity of the rules supposes that what makes the rules be universal is certain computational processes in the mind. That is, cognitive science says that in order to explain why all natural languages are done as to the same patterns of rules and those rules are such and not others, we are to investigate the activity of the brain as making certain computational procedures by analogy of those taking place in computers – generating of the rules is due to certain algorithms peculiar to the mind's computational processes. To clear up what processes it might be is certainly a purely empirical task.

Both in the case of studying the uniform syntactical structures of different natural languages and in the case where we are trying to establish what we suppose is behind this uniformity – namely, the computational processes of mind; our tasks are empirical. This means that whatever suppositions we make, trying to cope with those tasks, all those suppositions are to be experimentally tested, their truth or falsehood must be known from the corresponding empirical data; and if we wish at all to know whether suppositions are true or false, we should make only those suppositions on the syntactical structures and on the computational processes, whose truth or falsehood may be tested experimentally – only those suppositions have any sense as the ones on the structures or on the processes. In other words, again, as being empirical, both the universal grammar and what it is supposed to be behind it, cognitive science, must be falsifiable.

But let us turn now to certain suppositions which might seem "grammatical" in the usual sense, that are somehow able to be explained by (or appertain to) the "syntactical structures" of the universal grammar or presented as the products of the computational processes of the mind. We mean the assumptions "the meaning of a term changes when grammatically connected to another term, no matter similar or not" or "the term A grammatically connected to the term A may be anything but A". Can those assumptions for the reason that they are saying of the grammatical connection be presented as or be deduced from the statements of the universal grammar or be intended to be somehow yielded from the algorithms which rule the computational processes of the mind? In other words, can the universal grammar or cognitive science explain the ideas they support?

Evidently we must respond in the negative.

The motto of the Grammar of language (as we understand the word) "A and A is anything but A" has served to point out that no iteration of the instances of a law could with necessity lead to further iterations, for in the language with the

Grammar (natural language is counted to be such) iteration can only signify that the iterated has another meaning, hence may have another reference (earlier we have expressed the same thought in terms of the entities and systems of distinctions). Thus, despite that there are laws which fulfill without exceptions, of no law can be *said* that its everlasting fulfillment can take place. But if we cannot say that we can conclude further fulfillment of instances from their iterations, all we can do is to assert that a law may be *said* to be fulfilled in face of the iterations when there is no instance of which may be said that it contradicts the facts which are iterating. In other words, further instances may turn out to be *anything* except for the instances have been iterated (A and A may be *anything* but A), thus all that can be counted as the validity of a law is lack of anything but the iterating fact. This way we have come from the concept of the Grammar to the idea of falsifiability.

If we count the assertions of the Grammar of language as the ones (or on the same level as) of the universal grammar or cognitive science, then we must admit that those assertions must be empirically tested, and hence must be falsifiable. But in that case we have to falsify that in whose terms falsifiability may be established, which is not possible. To falsify that from which falsifiability itself may be inferred is simply circular.

The assertions of the Grammar of language are not of empirical character. Those assertions themselves determine how empirical data may be true. The assertions "A grammatically connected to A is anything but A" or "a term grammatically connected to another term changes its meaning" cannot be among the assertions of the universal grammar or those deduced by it. We cannot find any "theory" of this grammar which could be tantamount to those assertions and no "parameter" can signify terms to be such. What those statements assert is not falsifiable in the universal grammar. And it seems they cannot be corroborated by a computation proceeded in mind: we cannot connect any term of the computation and another such term to assert that to connect is to change a meaning because therefore the meaning must be changed as the result of *this* connection.

Entities in the Head

That the assertion that the meaning is changed by the grammatical connections is not a statement to pertain to the universal grammar and cannot be described with the help of the idea of the mental computational processes may seem to sound like a challenge. It looks as though an explorer was supposed to investigate a special "mental language" in which the mental processes proper or whatever was to be expressed to find out an analogue of the assumption that terms of language were distinct. Actually this assumption not only does not prompt to set up empirical tasks of that kind but it implies the contrary. Having assumed language to consist of the distinct terms, it seems, we have eventually to recognize that all such tasks are not decidable.

The assumption supposes that we cannot represent statements, words, thoughts in terms of any processes of the mind ultimately – that is, we cannot reduce natural language to some "mental language", algorithms, brain cells configurations or any descriptions of physiological processes or whatever without that this reduction itself is to be described in natural language.

This thought seems obvious and can be better explained by a very simple example. Suppose we are mastering some sort of such reductions, we could express anything in physiological terms, i.e. in terms of synapses and axons configurations or in no matter which terms concerning mental processes which could be supposed or discovered. We can set sensory data (or words, or thoughts) in correspondence with the elements of such a reduction. Suppose that for a horse (for the sensation of a horse perceived or the word "horse", no matter) there is the element of the reduction (so-to-say a bridge-term, the term with whose help the reduction is made), and it is ABC. In order to make the example more concrete we may say that we know that when we perceive some horse, in our brain there is the reaction ABC (suppose the reaction ABC is a certain configuration of brain cells, say, it is such-and-such coding in such-and-such area of the brain). And if the horse is, say, on the run, we have the reaction ABCD; if it is in the moonlight, the reaction ABCM; if it is painted by a brush, the reaction ABCP and so on – suppose we have a device allowing us to know instantly the reaction of the brain; whenever the object gets a property or characteristic, the device clarifies the according characteristic (the description in terms of the reduction) of the reaction of the brain.

But then, if we perceive the horse (barely, with no particular characteristic to be indicated by the device) and the device prompts it is ABC, we actually perceive the horse and ABC. We perceive the horse and the device makes us perceive ABC, since the processes in our brain for our perceiving the horse are ABC; so what we perceive is the horse and ABC. But this means that what the device must give on our perceiving the horse is not simply ABC, for the horse is ABC but the horse and ABC must give another reaction. It must be something peculiar to "the horse and ABC"; as well as ABC is peculiar to "the horse", ABCM is peculiar to "the horse in the moonlight" and so on.

What should our device give? Suppose "the horse and ABC" is ABCX. Thus having the device and perceiving the horse we should know that ABCX, i.e. that the perception of the horse and the perception of the expression of the "computation of the perception", namely ABC, is ABCX. But now our device must show the computational expression of the expression of the reaction to the perceiving of the horse (ABC) together with the formula for the reaction to the perceiving ABC (ABCX), which is obviously no ABC and no ABCX, this must be something which differs from each of them, this must be another configuration of brain cells (let us call it ABCXY). And this process must be repeated again and again (up to the infinite regress).

This means that it is not possible to provide a full correspondence between language (or its representation, i.e. the division of the reality into objects (and their properties) as in the language they may only be represented as such) and that which is supposed to generate language in the brain, i.e. processes of physical character which are responsible for the ability to speak and even for consciousness.

Any term or statement to be hypothetically generated by the corresponding mental processes must be regarded as grammatically connected to these processes ever since the processes are revealed and designated by a word, sign, sentence, etc.... In the language of distinct terms a term grammatically connected to another is anything but either of those terms. That is, if A is grammatically connected to B, then the yielded term AB is anything, but it is no A and no B (it may be designated as AB, or C, or D, etc.; but it would be a mistake to designate it as A or as B). Thus the term and the corresponding processes together must be something different than the term or the corresponding processes (the horse and ABC are neither the horse nor ABC, it is something different). And this new term must correspond to other processes than those to generate the previous term (this way we yield ABCX and so on). Connected terms are always different from those which are to be connected. The reason why we cannot strictly correspond our thought to the processes this thought is generated by is that in language connections of the terms generate other terms, different from the former; in other words, the reason is that connections change the meaning – the expressions which mean the process and the thought (or expression) which is supposed to be generated by the process have other meaning together than separately.

They have other meaning (the expression denoting a thought together with the generating processes has other meaning than the thought and other meaning than what is denoting the processes) because they have other sense and reference – a term (or the object which accords to the term in the representation of language peculiar for the object) and the corresponding brain processes may be regarded separately and together, as different entities and as the same entity (a thought or words may be regarded as nothing but the according brain processes and in some sense objects and irritations they produce is one and the same, for otherwise the irritations are not real or the existence of the objects is not proved). But we only can and do distinguish those entities just in the same way as we distinguish the terms denoting them – AB is anything but A and anything but B (in particular, AB is not A and AB is not B). Ontologically, it is by virtue of distinct entities that we cannot ultimately set the correspondence between language and the brain processes responsible for language. This correspondence engenders (speaking generally, it may be done in one way or other) new entities, distinct from those to be so corresponded.

The exact knowledge of the mental processes for which these or those thoughts or perceptions (conscious ones; those which we are expressing in words) must stand turns out to be impossible for the reason that in that case we would always have to find other processes to stand for the thoughts of the former processes. And this is due to the Grammar of language (or, in the upshot, to that which it is a part of and what it stands for, i.e. distinct entities); but up to now we did not emphasize that the Grammar may be regarded from this side – we have had to mention more often that AA is anything but A, instead of more general assertion that AB is anything but A and anything but B (AB is neither A nor B, no matter whether A is B or not).

Taken in its broad sense the mind-body problem is the questioning of the interaction of brain and consciousness, of the material and the mental, of language and what in the mind generates language. If we concentrate on the correspondence of a thought (the one which can be expressed in words) and what in the brain generates this thought, we take a very narrow approach to that problem. Besides, to say that a thought should correspond to what in the brain it generates means to say something merely hypothetical. Some may say that real mind-brain interactions may be more complicated than the hypothetical ones that consist in plain correspondences between some definite thoughts and the reactions or algorithms or configurations which are supposed to generate them. But no matter how the brain research may be carried out and what sophisticated methods may be thereby applied and what degree of complexity may be revealed, our speculation will hardly be concerned; for what is asserted in it is certain impossibility concerning the experiential approach in the field. We say that it is impossible to carry out a procedure where a thought may be corresponded to what it is generated by in the brain, for this very correspondence is creating another thought, different from the initial thought, which in its turn makes one think of other, different, correspondence. This is ruled by the fact that, in accordance with our conception, any connections generate something different from what is being connected, in the broad sense of the word.

If we regard this speculation as an approach to the mind-body problem, we should recognize that the problem having been taken in this narrow respect ("narrow" from the point of view of the range of aspects of the mind-body problem, but from the ontological point of view this is the broadest respect or the adequate one for the ontology) cannot be resolved.

Stating that it cannot be resolved we do not mean that there must be the mental and the physical and the former cannot be reduced to the latter. We may suppose that any or almost any mental phenomena can be explained in physiological terms – words, sensations, perceptions etc. accord to certain brain cells configurations; peculiarities of mental activity, such as diseases etc., are due to the peculiarities of physiological activity, etc. – and this will be corroborated by more and more precise experiments (which really takes place nowadays).

The problem cannot be resolved on the ontological level. Brain cells configurations must be different from the according words and perceptions as well as signs must be different from the objects they designate, or any object must be different from any once they are identified as such, or signs which are members of the assertion of identity must be different in general as different objects (different entities). Learning a new word we create a new configuration of the brain cells and learning which configuration it is we must create another configuration, but (and for this very reason) we cannot fully replace (or reduce) words by their configurations. Those two kinds of entities cannot be identical, and this is not just because they pertain to the two different kinds. But, in a sense, they are to pertain to the different kinds because they are to be distinct in such a world, as well as any entities are. The imaginary device which makes known which configuration corresponds to a word (or an impression) would perfectly carry out the idea of reductionism. And further considerations of how this device may function reveal that perfect reductionism is not possible for the ontological reasons.

Platonism

If the world consists of distinct entities, we cannot say of an entity that it exists without implying the existence of entities which are all distinct from the entity in question. Existence of something implies existence of what it is not.

And if this is so, suppose we name something. Then, in a sense, naming this, we must imply anything which is not this. For example, we say (or think or mean) "horse". Then knowing that it is impossible to exist and to be sole, we must imply, in a certain sense, anything what is not a horse, in particular that which can be a characteristic of a horse and that which cannot be its characteristic; that which has some relations to it and that which has no relation to it. Uttering "horse" we mean literally what we are uttering and, since there is nothing to exist sole, we mean, in general sense, all of which we know or can know that it is not what is uttered. And in this sense this is not absurd neither so surprising, for we cannot *speak* a word or an idea but we can speak language. Uttering "horse", we in the most general sense imply anything what we can say about a horse, or anything of what we can say that it could not be said about it.

Something which is singled out and not predicated may be regarded as general. It is general for the very reason that we do not inform anything about that, we give no details, no characteristic, and potentially this may be of *any* characteristic and of *any* predicate. This generality is not stipulated, as it is the case with categories of general or particular. When something is just uttered, the subject does not participate stating that it is general or particular, but it is general as it is, so to say, in an objective way. This kind of generality may be called language-dimensioned generality. Something which is just uttered is general for the very reason that it is not predicated, or, so to say, it is "predicated" by all language (or all the rest of language).

Thus, if we say "horse", it is general (in the sense of language-dimensioned generality). And if we say "the horse is mine", "the horse is black", ""horse" is a general concept", "a horse is a disguised demon" etc.; then it is not general (within the concept of language-dimensioned generality), but it is concretized, particularized, even if the generality (in categorical sense) is stipulated (language-dimensioned generality is the generality of a higher order).

What is just uttered (or may be just uttered) and is not predicated, singled out and not concretized, deserves the name of a universal. A universal is to what we may refer as having language-dimensioned generality, of which absolutely nothing special is said and of which anything what there is in language (except for that itself what is uttered) might be predicated. And this is based on the fact that, in view of the concept of the world as distinct entities, if anything can exist at all, it cannot exist alone. Entities are necessarily distinct from each other, and if the existence of an entity is established, this implies the existence of others; or if a concept is uttered, this implies the language-dimensioned generality of this concept (the existence of any other possible concept in language to predicate the uttered one).

If we understand universals this way, we may easily reject the objection of someone who says: "horse in general" cannot exist, for whenever I see a horse, I see a horse, but no horseness" (these speculations we have already mentioned at the very beginning of the work). We, in our turn, object to the ancient philosopher that whenever I see a horse, this is the horse which I see – in this case "horse" is always predicated, "detailed" by "I see". But horse in general, "horse" just uttered, is of generality which is dimensioned in language, is an entity which exists only as distinct from other entities, and cannot exist in any other way.

Thus we see that the concept of the world as distinct entities does not totally reject Platonism, as it might have seemed when we discussed our "rich man's argument". To contrary, it seems that this concept can be the basis for a construction of the idea of universals. It shows how this idea can be comprehended.

Needless to repeat that our views are the views of realists (this realism is, though, is not quite of customary understanding, as it is easy to notice). But this realism is the realism in modern sense of the word not in the medieval sense. But, in view of what we have just said of universals, are we *realists* (or *nominalists*) in the medieval sense of the word? In other words, having considered what we have just said about universals, can we assert that *universalia* are *ante rem* or that they are *post rem*?

Hardly could the question be answered strictly in the negative or strictly in the positive (and hardly ever was it correctly done so). All that we do introducing the notion of language-dimensioned generality is to reveal the way the notion of universals could be defined so that we could be able to consider them in *some sense* prior to things, or, roughly, we were trying to find out how words could be prior to things. And the notion of language-dimensioned generality implies that a thing, being distinct from others (which is their way to exist, as to our conception), must be characterized by its properties to clear up how it is distinct; and those properties must be named after the thing itself has –been named; so names are prior in the sense we are speaking about them in terms of the notion of language-dimensioned generality.

This notion implies any sign to be language-dimensioned – hence to be able to be regarded as a universal, if we just regard it as not grammatically connected. In particular, if we consider language-dimensioned generality, universals cannot be restricted to some part of speech; proper names can be regarded as universals; for a name (as well as any term) should firstly be regarded as a sign which potentially may designate anything, in any "possible world"; for it is grammatical connections that make of a sign a name or a predicate. Even if we know the definition of a sign (it is a word), it is implied to be already grammatically connected only as regards to this definition implied, hence it can be regarded as a universal – other connections are only "potential". It may be said even that anything recognized to be a sign may be regarded as a universal. Anything which is just a sign (no meaning is yet ascribed or just stipulated to be just a sign) is implied only to be distinct from whatever it could designate (from any possible referent). But this implies that a sign is nothing but an entity among other distinct entities. That is, it is possible to find a sense in which a word is prior to a thing just because signs are part of the world of such entities.

Bibliography

Anscombe.G.   *An Introduction to Wittgenstein's Tractatus.* London. 1957.
Ayer A.J.   *The Central Questions of Philosophy.* London. Weidenfeld & Nicolson. 1973.
The Foundations of Empirical Knowledge. London. Macmillan. 1961.
Language, Truth and Logic. Harmondsworth. Penguin Books. 1976.
Probability and Evidence. N.Y. Columbia Univ. Press. 1972.
The Problem of Knowledge. Harmondsworth. Penguin Books. 1972.
Barwise J. Ed.   *Handbook of Mathematical Logic.* Amsterdam.North-Holland.1978.
Brouwer L.E.J.   De onbetrouwbaarheid der logische principes, *Tijdschrift voor wijsbegeerte,* 2, 152-158. 1908.
Ueber die Bedeutung des Satzes vom asgeschlossenen Dritten in der Mathemetik, insbesondere in der Funktionentheorie, *Journal fur die reine und angewandte Mathematik,* 154 1-7, 1923.
Ueber Abbildung von Mannigfaltikeiten, *Math Annalen* 71, 97-115, 1912.
Cantor G.   *Contributions to the founding of the theory of transfinite numbers* ,Chicago&London, 1915.
Carnap R.   *The Logical Structure of the World.* Berkeley. Univ. Of California Press.1967.
The Logical Syntax of Language. London. Routledge & Kegan Paul.1967.
Meaning and Necessity. A Study in Semantics and Modal Logic. Chicago. Chicago Univ. Press. 1964.
Chomsky N.   *Aspects of the Theory of Syntax.* Cambridge. MIT. Press. 1976.
Language and the Problems of Knowledge. Cambridge. MIT. 1988.
New Horizons in the Study of Language and Mind. Cambridge Univ. Press.2000.

Churchland P. *Scientific Realism and the Plasticity of Mind.* Cambridge Univ. Press. 1979.
Le Cerveau: Moteur de la Reason, Siege de l'Ame. Paris. De Boeck Univ. 1999.
Cohen P. *Set Theory and the Continuum Hypothesis.* N.Y. Columbia Univ. Press. 1966.
Curry H. *Foundations of Mathematical Logic.* N.Y. Columbia Univ. Press. 1969.
Dummett M. *Frege: Philosophy of Language.* Cambridge. Harvard Univ. Press. 1981.
Frege : Philosophy of Mathematics. Cambridge. Harvard Univ. Press. 1991.
The Logical Basis of Metaphysics. Cambridge. Harvard Univ. Press. 1991.
Truth and Other Enigmas. Cambridge. Harvard. Univ. Press. 1978.
Fraenkel A. Bar-Hillel Y. *Foundations of Set Theory.* Amsterdam. 1958.
Frege G. *Translations from the Philosophical Writings of Gottlob Frege.* Oxford. Blackwell. 1952.
Fodor J.A. *The Language of Thought.* Cambridge. Harvard Univ. Press. 1979.
Representations: Philosophical essay on the Foundations of Cognitive Science. Cambridge. Harvard Univ. Press. 1981.
Goedel K. Die Vollstaendigkeit der Axiome des logischen Funktionenkalkuels, *Monatsch. Math. Phys.*, 37, 349-360. 1930.
Ueber formal Unentscheidbare Saetze der Principia Mathematica und verwandter Systeme, I, *Ibid.*, 38, 173-198. 1931.
The Consistency of the Axiom of Choice and of the Generalized Continuum Hypothesis. *Proc. Nat. Acad. Sci.*, 24, 556-557. 1938.
Consistency Proof for the Generalized Continuum Hypothesis, *Ibid.*, 25, 220-224. 1939.
The Consistency of the Axiom of Choice and the Generalized Continuum Hypothesis with the Axioms of Set Theory. *Annals of Mathematics Studies*, 3. Princeton, Princeton Univ. Press. 1940.
Hilbert D. Bernays P. *Grundlagen der Mathematik.* Berlin. 1934.
Heyting *A* *Intuitionism.* Amsterdam. North-Holland. 1956.
Kleene S.C. *Introduction to Metamathematics.* Van Nostrad, Prinston. 1952.
Kripke S. *Wittgenstein on Rules and Private language.* Cambridge Univ. Press. 1982.
Kuratowski K. *Introduction to Set Theory and Topology.* Oxford. Pergamon Press. 1972.
Luce R. Raiffa H. *Games and Decisions.* N.Y. Wiley & Sons. 1967.
Popper. K. *The Logic of Scientific Discovery.* N.Y. Basic Books. 1959.
Conjectures and Refutations. The Growth of Scientific Knowledge. London. Routledge. 1963.
Open Society and Its Enemies. N.Y. Harper & Row Publishers. 1963.
Putnam H. *Realism and Reason.* Cambridge Univ. Press. 1983.
Quine W.v O. *Elementary Logic.* Cambridge. Harvard Univ. Press. 1980.
Methods of Logic. Cambridge. Harvard Univ. Press. 1982.

Bibliography

	The ways of Paradox. Cambridge. Harvard Univ. Press. 1971.
	Mathematical Logic. N.Y. Norten. 1946.
	Set theory and Its Logic. Cambridge. Belkap Press. 1969.
	Word and Object. Cambridge. MIT Press. 1964.
	From the Logical Point of View. Cambridge. MIT. 1953.
	Ontological Relativity and Other Essays. N.Y. Columbia Univ.Press.1969.
Ramsay F.P.	The Foundations of Mathematics, *Proc. London Math. Soc.*, ser. 2, 25, 338-384. 1926.
Russell B.	*Introduction to Mathematical Philosophy.* London & N.Y. G. Allen and Unwin & McMillan. 1919.
Russell B. Whitehead A..	*Principia Mathematica.* Cambridge Univ. Press. 1910.
Tarski A.	*Logic, Semantic, Mathematics.* Oxford. Calderon Press. 1956.
Searle J.	*Expressions and Meaning.* Cambridge Univ. Press. 1979.
	Intentionality; An essay in the philosophy of mind. Cambridge Univ. Press. 1983.
	Speech Acts: An essay in the philosophy of language. Cambridge Univ. Press.1970.
Smullyan R.	*Theory of Formal Systems.* Prinston. Ptinston Univ. Press. 1961.
Wang Hao.	*A Survey of Mathematical Logic.* Peking. 1962.
Wittgenstein L	*Philosophical Investigations.* Oxford. Blackwell. 1989.
	Philosophical Remarks. Chicago Univ. Press. 1984.
	Preliminary Studies for the "Philosophical Investigations" ("blue and brown books") N.Y. Harper & Row. 1965.
	Tractatus Logico-Philosophicus. N.Y. Routledge & Kegan Paul. 1955.
	Wiener Ausgabe. Wien. Springer Verlag. 1993.
Wright C.	*Wittgenstein on the Foundations of Mathematics.* Cambridge. Harvard Univ. Press.1980.
	Realism, Meaning and Truth. Oxford. Blackwell. 1993.
Wright G.H.von.	*Causality and Determinism.* N.Y. Columbia Univ. Press. 1974.
	The Logical Problem of Induction. Oxford. Blackwell. 1957.
	Philosophical Logic. Ithaca. Cornell Univ. Press. 1984.
	Truth, Knowledge and Modality. Oxford. Blackwell. 1984.

Name Index

Anscombe 147
Ayer 147
Bar-Hillel 46, 147
Barwise 148
Bernayse 147
Brouwer 54, 73-75, 147
Cantor 7-11, 46, 147
Chomski 147
Churchland 147
Cohen 40, 147
Curry 88, 148
Dummett 147
Fodor 148
Frege 26, 43, 71, 147
Fraenkel 44, 46, 48, 147
Heraclites 107-109
Heyting 148
Hilbert 29-30, 147
Kleene 148

Kripke 127, 147
Kuratowski 35-36, 73, 147
Luce 147
Popper 107, 109, 119, 148
Putnam 148
Quine 9, 12, 47, 149
Raiffa 149
Ramsey 14, 149
Russell 7, 11-12, 47-48, 149
Searle 149
Smullyan 149
Tarski 149
von Wright 149
Wang Hao 32, 51, 149
Whitehead 149
Wittgenstein 73, 80-85, 127, 149
Wright C. 149
Zermello 11-12

Subject Index

addition 17-19
 cardinal 8-9, 38-40
Continuum Hypothesis 38-40
definiendum, definiens 17-18, 21
empty set or zero-sign 12, 64-65, 74,77
Euclidean space 69, 73
falsifiability 131-137
fixed point theorem 73, 74-75
formal arithmetic 29-31, 40,62
Goedel's theorem 30
grammatical connection 4, 7, 13, 14, 22, 27, 43, 51, 53, 57-58 ,59 ,69 ,118
intuitionism 54, 56, 148
"the term indistinguishable among its own kind" 64
Kuratowski's theorem 35-36
language-dimensioned generality 144-145
meta-language 1, 80, 102
metaphysics 93, 112,
mind-body problem 141-142
modus ponens, modus tollens 50, 58
non-linearity of natural language 88
object-language 1
ordinal 10, 13, 51
paradoxes 7
- logical 7-15
- semantical 43-52

Peano axioms 26, 29, 30-31
"Platonists" 7-15
quantum mechanics 104, 118
realism 101-102, 129, 144
set 7-15
set theories 7-14
skepticism 125-130, 135
-Humean 125-126
-modern 130
solipsism 83-84, 102
special relativity theory 103
syllogism 58, 62
The Copenhagen interpretation 115-119
distinct entities 96, 97, 111, 135, 148
the distinguishing function 71-72
the Grammar 1-5
the laws of logic 53-56
the paradox of language 85-86
-the metaphysical solution of 93-94
- the ontological solution of 95-97
the natural numbers 21-23
theory of types 12
topological space 65, 76, 85, 103
 universal grammar 135-137, 139
universals 14, 144-145
univocality 1, 17
Wittgenstein's language 79-81

www.ingramcontent.com/pod-product-compliance
Lightning Source LLC
Chambersburg PA
CBHW021832300426
44114CB00009BA/411